Medical Spanish

A *Pronto* Reference & Study Guide

Tara Bradley Williams

PRONTO
SPANISH

ISBN: 978-1-934467-74-9

All inquiries should be addressed to:
Pronto Spanish Services, LLC
P.O. Box 92
Lake Mills, WI 53551
www.ProntoSpanish.com

Table of Contents

Introduction

Welcome to **Medical Spanish: A *Pronto* Reference & Study Guide**. The Spanish word *pronto* means "quickly" or "promptly". The title is not meant to suggest that you will learn the entire Spanish language quickly. That would obviously take years and most likely, a significant amount of time in a Spanish-speaking country. Rather, *pronto* in this case is trying to help you solve your problem quickly. You may be an ER doctor that needs to communicate until the Spanish interpreter arrives. You may be a nurse in a clinic with several Spanish-speaking patients. You may be a front-desk receptionist checking in Spanish-speaking patients. Whatever your situation, you would like to know a bit more Spanish vocabulary.

Section 1: Spanish Fundamentals

This *Pronto* Reference & Study Guide was designed to first give you the basics. If you are brand new to the language or it has been a while since you have taken Spanish, I have included ways for you to practice with a friend or colleague. If you already know these words and phrases, just skim through it and go on to Section 2: Health Care Spanish Voabulary.

Section 2: General Health Care Spanish

This section starts to move you into more medical vocabulary to give you additional autonomy in learning the words and phrases you need. Some lists contain just vocabulary words. Other lists contain phrases and questions that you may be useful in your job. It will certainly not cover every situation, but it will give you a start to learning basic medical vocabulary in Spanish. Each section was intentionally designed with a lot of "white space." Think about your role working with Spanish-speakers. What vocabulary and phrases are missing? Use that white space to write down what vocabulary and phrases you need for your particular position.

Section 3: Specialty Spanish

The last section provides more specialty vocabulary. Look through this section and highlight words and phrases that you may say in your job. Note that this section also includes and entire blank page after each vocabulary list to allow you to write down words and phrases that you still need for your job, but may not be included in *the Pronto Reference & Study Guide*. If you would like to see specific words or phrases added, please feel free to contact me so that I can add it in the next edition.

Studying and memorizing vocabulary words only go so far, so make sure that you take these phrases and put them to use! I have yet to run into a Spanish-speaker who does not appreciate any effort that helps to bridge the language barrier. Most important, have fun on the Spanish language learning journey!

Tara Bradley Williams
Lake Mills, Wisconsin (December, 2015)

Section 1: Spanish Fundamentals

If you have ever taken a Spanish class before, chances are that you already know the majority of the words in this Section. If that is the case, just skim through this section quickly. Remember to highlight and write in words and phrases that may be useful to you.

If this is your very first time learning Spanish, find a partner to practice with or make flashcards. Better yet, use a free online flashcards service like www.quizlet.com that already has many of these lists made for you! Every chance you get, try using your new Spanish words and vocabulary. After all, the reason you want to learn Spanish is to communicate! Trust me when I say that the Spanish-speakers that you work with will truly enjoy helping you improve your Spanish. So have fun with it!

Spanish Alphabet

Let's start out right from the beginning with the alphabet. The letters *ch*, *ll*, *ñ* and *rr* are in addition to our English alphabet. Three of these letters, *ch*, *ll*, and *rr*, are no longer considered "official" letters according to the *Real Academia Española*, but some students still learn them. Only the *ñ* still has its own entry in the modern Spanish dictionary.

The other thing you may notice is that if you have taken Spanish before, you may have learned another word for the letter *w*. There are actually a few different ways that this letter can be said, depending on the region. One of the reasons for this is because the letter *W* (and *K*) are not native to the Spanish language and only show up in foreign words, such as *sitio web* (website), *waterpolo,* and *karate.*

Spanish Alphabet

A	a	*ah*		**N**	ene	*AY-nay*
B	be	*bay*		**Ñ**	eñe	*AY-nyay*
C	ce	*say*		**O**	o	*oh*
CH	che	*chay*		**P**	pe	*pay*
D	de	*day*		**Q**	cu	*koo*
E	e	*ay*		**R**	ere	*AY-ray*
F	efe	*AY-fay*		**RR**	erre	*AY-ray (trilled)*
G	ge	*hay*		**S**	ese	*AY-say*
H	hache	*AH-chay*		**T**	te	*tay*
I	i	*ee*		**U**	u	*oo*
J	jota	*HO-tah*		**V**	ve	*bay*
K	ka	*kah*		**W***	uve doble	*OO-bay DOH-blay*
L	ele	*AY-lay*		**X**	equis	*AY-keys*
LL	elle	*AY-yay*		**Y**	i griega	*ee gree-AY-gah*
M	eme	*AY-may*		**Z**	zeta	*SAY-tah*

*The letter "W" may also be said as doble u, doble v, uve dos, or doble uve, depending on the Spanish-speaking region.

Spanish Pronunciation

While there are some sounds that are definitely different in Spanish, overall, Spanish pronunciation is fairly easy. With a little bit of practice and following the same Spanish pronunciation rules, you will be able to pronounce any Spanish word. The Spanish vowels are the key to pronouncing the Spanish language correct. As in English, there are five vowels. Unlike English, these five vowels only make five different vowel sounds.

A	=	pronounced "ah"
E	=	pronounced "ay"
I	=	pronounced "ee"
O	=	pronounced "oh"
U	=	pronounced "oo"

Most of the consonant sounds are the same in Spanish as in English. For example, a "t" and "m" sound the same in Spanish. Below are a few of the exceptions.

C	"s" sound *(after an "e" or "i")*	**Ñ**	"ny" sound
G	"h" sound *(after an "e" or "i")*	**QU**	"k" sound
H	silent	**RR**	"r" sound *(trilled)*
J	"h" sound	**V**	"b" sound
LL	"y" sound *(some regions pronounce with a "j" sound)*	**Z**	"s" sound

Spanish Pronunciation Tips

- If a word has an accent mark, say that section of the word with more emphasis. (Practice: Mar<u>í</u>a, capit<u>án</u>, ro<u>mán</u>tico)

- If there is no accent mark on a word and it ends in a consonant, say the *last* part of the word with more emphasis. (Practice: espa<u>ñol</u>, do<u>lor</u>)

- If a word ends in a vowel, say the *second to last* part of the word with more emphasis. (Practice: am<u>i</u>go, <u>ta</u>co, fi<u>e</u>sta)

Grammar Tips

There are two ways to say "you" in Spanish – either informal (*tú*) or formal (*usted*). When you speak to someone you want to show respect to, such as your boss, a person you just met, or an older person, use the formal speech. When you are speaking to a family member, friend, or peer, you can use the informal speech.

Note that the literal translations of *me llamo* and *se llama* are "I call myself" and "he/she calls him/herself". However, this does not sound correct in English. Along these lines, as most beginners think in English, they want to add an extra *es* (is) in the sentence to make it *me llamo es*…. This is incorrect. You do not need *es* in this sentence. It is simply, *Me llamo (Tara).* (I call myself Tara.)

Greetings

Hello	Hola	*OH-la*
What is your name?	¿Cómo se llama? *(formal)*	*KO-mo say YAH-mah*
What is your name?	¿Cómo te llamas? *(informal)*	*KO-mo tay YAH-mahs*
My name is...	Me llamo...	*may YAH-moh*
Good morning.	Buenos días.	*BWAY-nose DEE-ahs*
Good afternoon.	Buenas tardes.	*BWAY-nahs TAR-days*
Good evening.	Buenas noches.	*BWAY-nose NO-chays*
How are you?	¿Cómo está? *(formal)*	*KO-mo ay-STAH*
How are you?	¿Cómo estás? *(informal)*	*KO-mo ay-STAHS*
How are you?	¿Qué tál? *(informal)*	*kay tahl*
Very well.	Muy bien.	*mwee bee-YEN*
Well.	Bien.	*bee-YEN*
Fine.	Más o menos.	*mahs o MAY-nose*
OK	Así así.	*ah-SEE ah-SEE*
Not well.	Mal.	*mahl*
Very badly.	Muy mal.	*mwee mahl*

Conversation Activities: Greetings

Hand Gestures: Come up with basic hand gestures for the responses to the questions *¿Cómo estás?* or *¿Qué tál?* For example: *Bien* = Thumbs up. *Muy bien* = Double thumbs up. Practice these gestures with your partner.

Have a basic conversation in Spanish.
Greet the person.
Ask his/her name.
Ask how he/she is doing.

Large Group Practice

Group Name Activity: First within pairs, one person asks another, *¿Cómo se llama?* and the person responds *Me llamo* _____. When the pairs know the others names, they combine with another pair (so now there are 4 people in a group). Do this until the entire group is together and can be identified by name. (Ex: *Me llamo Bob. Se llama Jim. Se llama Julie. Se llama Carrie.*)

Hot Potato: For more fun and interactivity, everybody forms a circle. One person throws a ball (or squishy stuffed animal) to another, asking his or her name. *(¿Cómo se llama?)* The person who caught the ball says his/her name. *(Me llamo* _____.*)* That person throws to someone else, asking his or her name and so on. Add the question *¿Cómo está(s)?* to the game for more variety.

Conversation Phrases

Where are you from?	¿De dónde es? *(formal)*	*day DOAN-day ace*
Where are you from?	¿De dónde eres? *(informal)*	*day DOAN-day AIR-ays*
I'm from (Mexico).	Soy de (Mexico).	*soy day (MEH-hee-ko)*
Nice to meet you.	Mucho gusto.	*MOO-cho GOOSE-toh*
Goodbye.	Adiós.	*ah-dee-OSE*
See you later.	Hasta luego.	*AH-stah loo-WAY-go*
Until I see you again.	Hasta la vista.	*AH-stah la BEE-stah*
What's up?	¿Qué pasa?	*kay PAH-sah*
All's well.	Todo bien.	*TOH-doh bee-YEN*
Nothing.	Nada.	*NAH-dah*

Conversation Activities: Conversation Phrases

Where are you from? Practice the conversation phrase, *¿De dónde eres?* (or *¿De dónde es?*), as well as "goodbyes".

Have a basic conversation in Spanish.
Greet the person
Ask his/her name
Ask how he/she is doing
Ask where he/she is from
Say goodbye

Large Group Practice:
Make sure everybody in the group knows everybody's name. Somebody starts asking another, *¿De dónde es?* (or *¿De dónde eres?*). The person responds, *Soy de ___.* That person asks the next person in the group and adds on to the conversation. Such as, *Me llamo Tara. Soy de Evansville. Se llama Jim. Es de Colorado.* Keep going until everybody's name has been asked and where they are from.

Survival Words

How do you say...?	¿Cómo se dice...?	*KO-mo say DEE-say*
What does...mean?	¿Qué significa...?	*kay seeg-nee-FEE-kah*
I don't understand.	No comprendo/No entiendo.	*no comb-PRAIN-doh/no ain-TYEN-doh*
I don't know.	No sé.	*no say*
Do you speak English?	¿Habla(s) inglés?	*AH-blah(s) in-GLACE*
Do you speak Spanish?	¿Habla(s) español?	*AH-blah(s) ace-pahn-YOLE*
Do you read English?	¿Lee(s) inglés?	*LAY-ay(s) een-GLACE*
Do you write English?	¿Escribe(s) inglés?	*ace-KREEB-ay(s) een-GLACE*
Yes	Sí	*see*
A little	Un poco	*oon PO-koh*
Very little	Un poquito	*oon po-KEY-toh*
No	No	*no*
Repeat, please.	Repita, por favor.	*ray-PEE-tah por fah-BORE*
Pardon me	Perdón.	*pair-DOAN*

Grammar Tip

*Add an "s" to the end of a verb to make it informal (*tú*) when speaking to peers, family, and friends.

Conversation Activities: Survival Words

¿Cómo se dice? Point to items in the room and ask *¿Cómo se dice...?* The other person answers if he/she knows the Spanish word. If not, the person will answer *no sé.* (Make sure to look up the word you do not know in an online dictionary, such as www.WordReference.com, if it is necessary for your job.)

¿Qué significa...? Find a Spanish word that you do not know (in an online Spanish article, Spanish-English dictionary, or look ahead in the book). Ask what the word means by saying *¿Qué significa...?* The other person answers in English if he/she knows the meaning. If not, the person will answer *no sé* (I don't know).

Have a basic conversation in Spanish.
> Greet the person.
> Ask his/her name.
> Ask if he/she speaks English/Spanish.
> Ask if he/she reads English/Spanish.
> Ask how he/she is doing.
> Ask where he/she is from.
> Say goodbye.

Numbers 0-10

0	cero	*SAIR-oh*
1	uno	*OON-oh*
2	dos	*dose*
3	tres	*trace*
4	cuatro	*KWAH-troh*
5	cinco	*SEEN-koh*
6	seis	*sase*
7	siete	*see-AY-tay*
8	ocho	*OH-choh*
9	nueve	*NWAY-bay*
10	diez	*dee-ACE*

Conversation Activities: Numbers 0-10

Answer these questions using Spanish numbers.

What is your phone number?

What is your street address?

What is the address of your place of employment?

What is your zip code?

How many people are in your family?

How many people are in the room right now?

How many pets do you have?

What numbers and letters are on your license plate? (A good expression to know here is, *¡Ni idea!* - No idea.)

Using the Spanish numbers 0-10, count:

Backwards (diez to cero)

Even numbers forward

Even numbers backward

Odd numbers forward

Odd numbers backward

Large Group Practice: Play *Go Fish!* (Google the directions if you have forgotten how to play this game.) Using the cards 2-9, ask your friends *¿Tiene...?* (Do you have....?) The person will respond with either *Sí, tengo...* or *No, no tengo...* If the person does not have the number you are looking for, tell them to "Go Fish!" - *"¡A Pescar!"*

Numbers 11-1000

11	once	*OWN-say*
12	doce	*DOH-say*
13	trece	*TRAY-say*
14	catorce	*kah-TORE-say*
15	quince	*KEEN-say*
16	dieciséis	*dee-ace-ee-SASE*
17	diecisiete	*dee-ace-ee-see-AY-tay*
18	dieciocho	*dee-ace- ee-OH-choh*
19	diecinueve	*dee-ace-ee-NWAY-bay*
20	veinte	*BAIN-tay*
30	treinta	*TRAIN-tah*
40	cuarenta	*kwah-RAIN-tah*
50	cincuenta	*seen-KWEHN-tah*
60	sesenta	*say-SANE-tah*
70	setenta	*say-TANE-tah*
80	ochenta	*oh-CHAIN-tah*
90	noventa	*no-BANE-tah*
100	cien/ciento	*see-AIN/see-AIN-toh*
1000	mil	*meel*

Grammar Tip

*Note that *cien* is only used for the number 100. Use *ciento* for numbers 101-199.

Conversation Activities: Numbers 11-1000

Numbers not ending in 0. To say numbers that do not end in 0, simply add a "*y*" (meaning "and") and the single digit number. Examples: 33 = *treinta y tres,* 78 = *setenta y ocho,* 52 = *cincuenta y dos.* To practice, one person says a 2-digit number in English and the other says what it is in Spanish.

Math: Create math problems for one another. One person says the number and the other writes it down and solves the math problem. (+ *más,* - *menos,* = *son*) Example: 12 + 11 = 23 would translate to *doce más once son veinte y tres.*

Saying the price. Point to an object in the room and ask your partner about how much it costs. Example: ¿*Cuánto cuesta el libro?* (How much does the book cost?) *Cuesta diez dólares.* (It costs $10.)

Answer these questions in Spanish:
How old do you have to be in order to drive?
How old do you have to be to drink alcohol?
How old are you now?
How old are you going to be when you retire?
Write your 10-digit phone number down. Say the number in pairs (which is very common among Spanish-speakers). Example: 999-222-1234 would be written and said as 99-92-22-12-34.

Colors

red	rojo	*ROW-hoe*
blue	azul	*ah-SOOL*
green	verde	*BARE-day*
yellow	amarillo	*ah-mar-EE-yoh*
white	blanco	*BLAHN-koh*
black	negro	*NAY-groh*
purple	morado	*more-AH-doh*
pink	rosado	*roh-SAH-doh*
orange	naranja/anaranjado	*nar-AHN-ha/ah-nar-ahn-HA-doh*
brown	café/pardo/marrón	*kah-FAY/PAR-doh/mar-RONE*

Some ideas to help you remember:
verde: Like Mesa Verde ("Green Table") in Colorado
amarillo: Like Amarillo, TX
café: Like the word for coffee
blanco: Like a blank sheet of paper

Conversation Activities: Colors

Identify the Colors of Items Around You. Ask what color something is with the question, *¿De qué color es ___?*

> *Note that there are 4 ways to say "the" in Spanish. If the noun is singular (one thing), use "el" (masculine noun) or "la" (femine noun). If the noun is plural (two or more things), use "los" (masculine) or "las" (feminine).*

You would answer this question with *Es* or *Son* (<u>color name</u>).

Examples:
La cama es blanca. (The bed is white.)
El libro es negro. (The book is black.)
Las camas son blancas. (The beds are white.)
Los libros son negros. (The books are black.)

Noun/Adjective Placement: In Spanish, the adjective (color) goes after the object and also matches in number and gender. Practice having the noun and the color "match". For example: *el libro verde/los libros verdes* (the green book/the green books); *la mesa blanca/las mesas blancas* (the white table/the white tables). Here are some nouns to get you going:

 la casa (the house)
 la silla (the chair)
 la pluma (the pen)
 el edificio (the building)
 el plato (the plato)
 el cuaderno (the notebook)

Directions

Where is...?	¿Dónde está...?	*DOAN-day ay-STAH*
Continue...	Siga...	*SEE-gah*
Turn...	Doble...	*DOH-blay*
Go...	Vaya a...	*BYE-yah ah*
It is...	Está...	*ay-STAH*
to the right	a la derecha	*ah la dare-AY-chah*
to the left	a la izquierda	*ah la ease-key-AIR-dah*
straight ahead	recto/derecho	*RAKE-toh/dare-AY-choh*
under/below	debajo de	*day-BAH-hoe day*
over/on top of	encima de	*en-SEE-mah day*
next to	al lado de	*ahl LAH-doh day*
in front of	delante de	*day-LAHN-tay day*
behind	detrás de	*day-TRAHS day*
close to	cerca de	*SAIR-kah day*
far from	lejos de	*LAY-hoes day*
here	aquí	*ah-KEY*
there	allá/allí	*ah-YAH/ah-YEE*
very close	muy cerca	*mwee SAIR-kah*
very far	muy lejos	*mwee LAY-hohs*

Conversation Activities: Directions

Walking Directions: From where you are, give walking directions to the:
    bathroom (*el baño)*
    kitchen (*la cocina*)
    entrance *(la entrada)*
    common place of your choosing

Driving Directions: From where you are, give driving directions to the:
    grocery store (*el supermercado*)
    gas station (*la gasolinera*)
    school (*la escuela*)
    park (*el parque*)

Spatial Relationships: Take a pen (*la pluma*) and place it on a table (*la mesa*). Practice giving sentences that describe the pen in relationship to the table. For example: *La pluma está encima de la mesa.* (The pen is over the table.) *La pluma está debajo de la mesa.* (The pen is under the table.)

Large Group Activity: Put on some blindfolds and go on a Trust Walk. One person leads another (with a blindfold on), giving directions only in Spanish.

Question Words

What?	¿Qué?	*kay*
How?	¿Cómo?	*KOH-moh*
How much?	¿Cuánto?	*KWAHN-toh*
When?	¿Cuándo?	*KWAHN-doh*
Which?	¿Cuál?	*kwahl*
Who?	¿Quién?	*key-AIN*
Why?	¿Por qué?	*pore KAY*
Where?	¿Dónde?	*DOAN-day*

Conversation Activities: Questions

Brainstorm: Come up with some questions that you already know with these words. For example, fill in what comes to mind: *¿Cómo...? ¿Dónde...?*

More Brainstorming with Questions: Try coming up with a sentence for each question word. See if your partner or group can answer it. (Don't worry. At this point, I expect a lot of *Spanglish*! I am just trying to get you to talk, and at the beginning without a lot of vocabulary, it is hard!)

Large Group Activity: As a group, see if you can come up with "tricks" that will help you remember the differences between the question words. (For example: How can you remember the difference between *cuándo* and *cuánto?*)

Time

What time is it?	¿Qué hora es?	*kay ORE-ah ace*
It is 1:00.	Es la una.*	*Ase la OO-nah*
It is 3:00 PM.	Son las tres de la tarde.	*sone las trace day la TAR-day*
It is 10:06 AM.	Son las diez y seis de la mañana.	*sone las dee-AYS ee sase day la mah-NYAH-nah*
It is 8:15 PM.	Son las ocho y cuarto de la noche.	*sone las OH-choh ee KWAR-toh day la NO-chay*
It is 5:30.	Son las cinco y media.	*sone las SEEN-koh ee MAY-dee-ah*
At what time?	¿A qué hora?	*ah kay ORE-ah*
At 4:00.	A las cuatro.	*ah las KWAH-troh*
noon	mediodía	*may-dee-oh-DEE-ah*
midnight	medianoche	*may-dee-ah-NO-chay*
in the morning	de la mañana	*day la mah-NYAH-nah*
in the afternoon	de la tarde	*day la TAR-day*
at night	de la noche	*day la NO-chay*

* Note: "*Es*" is only used in the 1 o'clock hour.

Conversation Activities: Time

Time: Write down a time for your partner and ask him/her, *¿Qué hora es?*

Answer these questions:
> ¿Qué hora es?
>
> ¿A qué hora se levanta (wake up)?
>
> ¿A qué hora empieza a trabajar (begin working)?
>
> ¿A qué hora...? (Fill in the blank.)

Large Group Practice: Make a clock out of a paper plate, a pin, and two "hands". One person stands in front of the group and gives several examples for the others to say what time it is.

Months and Seasons

January	enero	*ay-NAIR-oh*
February	febrero	*fay-BRARE-oh*
March	marzo	*MAR-soh*
April	abril	*ah-BREEL*
May	mayo	*MY-yoh*
June	junio	*HOO-nee-oh*
July	julio	*HOO-lee-oh*
August	agosto	*ah-GO-stoh*
September	septiembre	*saip-tee-AIM-bray*
October	octubre	*oak-TOO-bray*
November	noviembre	*no-bee-AIM-bray*
December	diciembre	*dee-see-AIM-bray*
Spring	primavera	*preem-ah-BARE-ah*
Summer	verano	*bare-AH-noh*
Fall	otoño	*oh-TONE-nyoh*
Winter	invierno	*een-bee-AIR-noh*
What is today's date?	¿Cuál es la fecha de hoy?	*KWAHL es la FAY-cha day oy*
Today is the (2nd of March).	Hoy es el (2 de marzo).	*oy es el (dose day MAR-so)*

Note that the months of the year are **not** capitalized in Spanish.

Conversation Activities: Months and Seasons

Months: Say the 12 months in order. You can either say these individually or go back in forth with a partner trying to say them all in order.

Today's Date: Ask your partner today's date. *¿Cuál es la fecha de hoy?* Answer: *Hoy es el (day) de (month).*

If the question applies, ask your partner the following:
    ¿Cúando es su cumpleaños? (When is your birthday?)
    ¿Cúando es su aniversario? (When is your anniversary?)
    ¿Cúando es el cumpleaños de su hijo? (When is your son's birthday?)
    ¿Cúando es...? (Fill in the blank.)

Ask the date for various holidays. Either say the English word or look it up on www.WordReference.com. Example: *¿Cuándo es Navidad?* or *¿Cuál es la fecha de Navidad?* Answer: *Navidad es el 25 de diciembre.*

Days of the Week and Date

Monday	lunes	*LOO-nays*
Tuesday	martes	*MAR-tays*
Wednesday	miércoles	*mee-AIR-cole-ays*
Thursday	jueves	*hoo-AY-bays*
Friday	viernes	*bee-AIR-nays*
Saturday	sábado	*SAH-bah-doh*
Sunday	domingo	*doh-MEAN-go*
week	semana	*say-MAH-nah*
weekend	fin de semana	*feen day say-MAH-nah*
When is...?	¿Cuándo es...?	*KWAHN-doh ace*
Monday, February 8	lunes, el ocho de febrero	*LOO-nays, el OH-choh day fay-BRAY-oh*

Note that the days of the week are **not** capitalized in Spanish and that the Spanish week starts on a Monday.

Conversation Activities: Days of the Week & Date

Days of the Week: Say the seven days of the week in order. You can either say these individually, or go back in forth with a partner trying to say them all in order. (Remember that the Spanish week starts on a Monday.)

Today, Tomorrow, and Yesterday: Ask your partner the name of the day for today, tomorrow, and yesterday.

¿Qué día es hoy (today)?

¿Qué día es mañana (tomorrow)?

¿Qué día fue ayer (was yesterday)?

Ask basic questions regarding the week, such as:

¿Cuál es tu día favorito?

¿Cuándo trabajas (work)?

¿Cuándo es el fin de semana (weekend)?

Family

Who is this?	¿Quién es?	*key-AIN ace*
He/she is my…	Él/ella es mi…	*ell/AY-yah ace mee*
spouse	esposo/a	*ay-SPOH-soh/sah*
husband	marido	*mah-REE-doh*
wife	mujer	*moo-HARE*
father	padre	*PAH-dray*
mother	madre	*MAH-dray*
brother	hermano	*air-MAH-noh*
sister	hermana	*air-MAH-nah*
son	hijo	*EE-hoe*
daughter	hija	*EE-hah*
grandfather	abuelo	*ah-BWAY-loh*
grandmother	abuela	*ah-BWAY-lah*
grandson	nieto	*nee-AY-toh*
granddaughter	nieta	*nee-AY-tah*
uncle	tío	*TEE-oh*
aunt	tía	*TEE-ah*
nephew	sobrino	*so-BREE-noh*
niece	sobrina	*so-BREE-nah*
cousin	primo/a	*PREE-moh*

Conversation Activities: Family

Describe who is in your family. For example: *Frank es mi padre. Bobbie es mi madre. Carrie es mi hermana. Joe y Adam son mis hermanos.*

Small Talk: Now that you know a bit more about your group's families, let's practice our small talk and ask how they are. For example, *¿Cómo está su padre?* (You could answer, *Mi padre está bien.*)

Clarification: Maybe you want to clarify the name of the mother, so you could ask, *¿Cómo se llama su madre?* (You would answer, *Mi madre se llama Roberta.*)

CULTURAL NOTE: In many Spanish speaking countries, people have two last names - their father's last name and their mother's last name. Women often do not change their names once they get married. For children, the father's last name goes first (in the space where in the traditional U.S. culture, we have our middle name). Therefore, if Juan Lopez (father's last name) Garcia (mother's last name) marries María Castillo (father's last name) Ayala (mother's last name), their child would be named Guadalupe Lopez Castillo.

Tell your group your name. What would your name be in the traditional Spanish way, with your first name, father's last name, and then mother's maiden name. If you have children, write down what their names would be.

Personal Characteristics

(dis)organized	(des)ordenado	*(day)sore-day-NAH-doh*
(im)patient	(im)paciente	*(eem)pah-see-AIN-tay*
artistic	artístico	*ar-TEE-stee-koh*
caring	cariñoso	*kar-een-YOH-soh*
funny	gracioso	*grah-see-OH-soh*
generous	generoso	*hane-air-OH-soh*
good-looking	guapo	*GWAH-poh*
hard-working	trabajador	*trah-bah-hah-DOOR*
intelligent	inteligente	*een-tail-ee-HANE-tay*
lazy	perezoso	*pare-ay-SOH-soh*
mean	antipático	*ahn-tee-PAH-tee-koh*
nice	simpático	*seem-PAH-tee-koh*
old	viejo	*bee-AY-hoh*
pretty	bonito	*boh-NEE-toh*
quiet	callado	*kie-AH-doh*
serious	serio	*SAIR-ee-oh*
short	bajo	*BAH-hoh*
tall	alto	*AHL-toh*
ugly	feo	*FAY-oh*
young	joven	*HAH-ben*

Grammar Tip

For males, keep the adjective with an *o* at the end. For females, replace the *o* and put an *a*.

For example:

Tomás es serio. Laura es graciosa.

Conversation Activities: Personal Characteristics

Opposites: See if you can find opposite pairs in the vocabulary list of personal characteristics. One person says a Spanish word (example: *ordenado*) and another says the opposite meaning (example: *desordenado*).

Describe People: Describe people and things using these new Spanish adjectives. Remember that in Spanish, the noun goes first and the adjective goes second. Also work on the gender and number, meaning that if the noun is feminine, put an "a" at the end of the adjective. If there is more than one object, put an "s" at the end of the adjective.

Examples:
Carla es alta. (Carla is tall.)
Ellas son altas. (They are tall.)
El libro es grande. (The book is big.)
Los libros son grandes. (The books are big.)
el hombre viejo (the old man)
la mujer vieja (the old woman)

Likes and Dislikes

I like (to)…	Me gusta…	*may GOO-stah*
You like (to)…	Le gusta…	*lay GOO-stah*
Do you like (to)…?	¿Le gusta…?	*lay GOO-stah*
Yes, I like (to)…	Sí, me gusta…	*see may GOO-stah*
No, I do not like (to)…	No, no me gusta…	*no no may GOO-stah*
What do you like to do?	¿Qué le gusta hacer?	*kay lay GOO-stah ah-SAIR*
read	leer	*lay-AIR*
eat	comer	*koh-MARE*
cook	cocinar	*koh-see-NAR*
play (a sport/game)	jugar al	*hoo-GAR ahl*
watch	mirar el	*meer-AR el*
basketball	baloncesto	*bah-lone-SAY-stoh*
baseball	béisbol	*BAYS-bole*
soccer	fútbol	*FOOT-bole*
football	fútbol americano	*FOOT-bole ah-mare-ee-KAH-noh*
golf	golf	*goalf*
watch TV	mirar la television	*meer-AR la tay-lay-bee-see-OWN*
go to the movies	ir al cine	*eer ahl SEE-nay*
play piano/guitar	tocar el piano/la guitarra	*toh-KAR el pee-AH-no/la gee-TAR-ah*
be with my family	estar con mi familia	*ay-STAR cone mee fah-MEE-lee-ah*
exercise	hacer ejercicio	*ah-SAIR ay-hair-SEE-see-oh*
travel	viajar	*bee-ah-HAR*

Conversation Activities: Likes and Dislikes

What do you like to do? One person asks the question, *¿Qué le gusta hacer?* The other person answers with all of the things that you like to do, starting with *Me gusta...* Go to an online dictionary, such as www.WordReference.com, to find the words you do not know.

What do you like? Look up foods and activities that you want to ask your partner about and say, *¿Le gusta...?* (Do you like..?) Your partner will answer with *Sí, me gusta....* or *No, no me gusta...*

Large Group Activity: One person will start out with something that he/she likes/dislikes. The next person will state what the first person says and then add on his/her like/dislike. Keep adding until everybody has their like/dislike included. If it is a smaller group, go around the group again to make it more complicated.

Examples:
Me gusta cocinar.
A Jane le gusta cocinar. Me gusta viajar.
A Jane le gusta cocinar. A Bob le gusta viajar. Me gusta golf.
A Jane le gusta cocinar. A Bob le gusta viajar. A Michael le gusta golf. Me gusta estar con mi familiar.

Continue to add more people and see how many your group can remember.

Clothing

What are you wearing?	¿Qué lleva puesto?	*kay YAY-bah PWAY-stoh*
I am wearing...	Llevo puesto...	*YAY-boh PWAY-stoh...*
shoes	los zapatos	*los sah-PAH-tohs*
pants	los pantalones	*los pahn-tah-LONE-ays*
dress	el vestido	*el bay-STEE-doh*
skirt	la falda	*la FAHL-dah*
shorts	los pantalones cortos	*los pahn-tah-LONE-ays CORE-tohs*
blouse	la blusa	*la BLUE-sah*
jacket	la chaqueta	*la chah-KAY-tah*
slippers	las zapatillas	*las sah-pah-TEE-yahs*
swimming suit	el traje de baño	*el TRAH-hay day BAH-nyo*
shirt	la camisa	*la kah-MEE-sah*
t-shirt	la camiseta	*la kah-mee-SAY-tah*
sweatshirt	la sudadera	*la soo-dah-DARE-ah*
socks	los calcetines	*los kahl-say-TEE-nays*
sweater	el suéter	*el SWAY-tare*

Conversation Activities: Clothing

Identify Clothing: Identify all that you and your partner are wearing by first asking the question, *¿Qué lleva puesto?* The person will respond with, *Llevo puesto…*

Identify Clothing and Color: For an added challenge, identify the color (an adjective) that goes with each article of clothing. Remember that the color goes after the clothing item. (For example: *una camisa roja* = a red shirt)

Grammar Note

Note that you can change the *"la"* (the) to *"una"* (a). Here's a quick look. The definite article, "the", turns into the indefinite article "a/some": el - una, la - una, los - unos, las - unas

For example:
la camisa (the shirt) – *una camisa* (a shirt)
el vestido (the dress) – *un vestido* (a dress)
las camisas (the shirts) – *unas camisas* (some shirts)
los vestidos (the dresses) – *unos vestidos* (some dresses)

Clothing Accessories

What do you have?	¿Qué tiene(s)?	*kay tee-AIN-ay(s)*
I have...	Tengo...	*TANG-goh*
Do you have...?	¿Tiene(s)...?	*tee-AIN-ay(s)...*
Yes, I have...	Sí, tengo...	*see TANG-goh...*
No, I don't have...	No, no tengo...	*no no TANG-goh...*
belt	el cinturón	*el seen-tour-OWN*
hat	el sombrero	*el sohm-BRAY-roh*
baseball hat	la gorra	*la GORE-ah*
ski cap	el gorro	*el GORE-oh*
umbrella	el paraguas	*el par-AH-gwahs*
glasses	las gafas *OR* los lentes	*las GAH-fahs OR los LANE-tays*
purse	el bolso	*el BOWL-soh*
tie	la corbata	*la core-BAH-tah*
gloves	los guantes	*los GWAHN-tays*
bracelet	la pulsera	*la pool-SAIR-ah*
earrings	los aretes *OR* los pendientes	*los ah-RAY-tays los pane-dee-AIN-tays*
necklace	el collar	*el koh-YAR*
wallet	la cartera	*la kar-TARE-ah*

Conversation Activities: Clothing Accessories

What is in your closet? Find out what the other person "has" in their closet by asking, *¿Qué tiene (en su clóset)?* Remember that for an extra challenge, you can put the color at the end of the clothing accessory. Example: *Tengo un cinturón negro.*

Do you have this particular item? Ask your partner if they have something in particular. For example: *¿Tiene un cinturón rojo?* (Do you have a red belt?)

Magazines/Ads: Find a magazine or ads that are advertising clothing. See how many clothing accessories you can identify.

Section 2: General Health Care Spanish

This section is probably the reason why you have this book! There are lots of ways you can learn the information in the Spanish Fundamentals section, but the Health Care Specific Spanish vocabulary is a bit harder to find.

These vocabulary lists are meant to get you started and are not all-inclusive. I have left plenty of white space for you to write your own vocabulary and phrases that you need. There are several places where you can find additional vocabulary you need for your job, but my favorite two places are the online dictionary www.WordReference.com and the paperback *Medical Dictionary/Diccionario Médico* by Glenn T. Rogers, MD.

Job Titles and People

I am (the)...	Soy (el/la)...	*soy (el/la)*
assistant	asistente	*ah-see-STEHN-tay*
boss	jefe	*HAY-fay*
dietician	dietista	*dee-ay-TEE-stah*
doctor	médico/doctor	*MAY-dee-koh/doke-TORE*
nurse	enfermero	*en-fair-MARE-oh*
pediatrician	pediatra	*pay-dee-AH-trah*
pharmacist	farmacéutico	*farm-ah-SAY-oo-tee-koh*
receptionist	recepcionista	*ray-sep-see-oh-NEE-stah*
specialist	especialista	*ay-spay-see-ah-LEE-stah*
supervisor	supervisor	*soo-pair-bee-SORE*
surgeon	cirujano	*seer-oo-HAH-noh*
technician	técnico	*TAKE-nee-koh*
therapist	terapeuta	*tare-ah-pay-OO-tah*
worker	trabajador	*trah-bah-hah-DOOR*

He/she is a...	Él/ella es un/una...	
baby	bebé	*bay-BAY*
boy/girl (*younger*)	niño/a	*NEE-nyoh/nyah*
boy/girl	chico/a	*CHEE-koh/kah*
inpatient	paciente interno	*pah-see-AIN-tay een-TARE-noh*
man	hombre	*OHM-bray*
outpatient	paciente externo	*pah-see-AIN-tay ex-TARE-noh*
patient	paciente	*pah-see-AIN-tay*
teenager	muchacho/a	*moo-CHAH-choh/chah*
visitor	visitante	*bee-see-TAHN-tay*
woman	mujer	*moo-HARE*

Conversation Activities: Job Titles and People

What is your job? Ask what someone does for a living by saying *¿Cuál es su profesión?* The person will answer with *Soy...* If your profession or job title is not in the list, make sure to look it up so that you can be ready when someone asks you.

Describe your co-workers. Think of a co-worker. What is his/her name? *¿Cómo se llama?* What is his/her job-title? *¿Cuál es su profesión?* You would answer, *Se llama... Es...*

Name 12 people. Looking at the list of 12 people on the previous page (*bebé, niño, niña*, etc.), name a person that fits into each category.

For example:
Olivia es una bebé.
Parker es un niño.
Erin es una niña.
Kevin es un chico.
Molly es una chica.

Parts of the Body - Face

What hurts?	¿Qué le duele?	*kay lay DWAY-lay*
My … hurts.	Me duele (el/la) ….	*may DWAY-lay (el/la)*
head	la cabeza	*la kah-BAY-sah*
face	la cara	*la KAR-ah*
chin	la barbilla	*la bar-BEE-yah*
cheeks	las mejillas	*las may-HEE-yahs*
ear (outer)	la oreja	*la ore-AY-hah*
ear (inner)	el oído	*el oh-EE-doh*
eye	el ojo	*el OH-hoh*
eyelashes	las pestañas	*las pay-STAHN-yahs*
eyelid	el párpado	*el PAR-pah-doh*
forehead	la frente	*la FRAIN-tay*
hair	el pelo	*el PAY-loh*
lips	los labios	*los LAH-bee-ohs*
mouth	la boca	*la BOW-kah*
neck	el cuello	*el KWAY-yoh*
nose	la nariz	*la nar-EES*
teeth	los dientes	*los dee-AIN-tays*
tongue	la lengua	*la LANE-gwah*

Conversation Activities: Parts of the Body - Face

Identify Parts of the Face: Start with one person in the group, point to a body part on the face, and say the Spanish name. The next person does the same. Continue to go around in a circle. See how many facial body parts you know as a group.

Write the Spanish words for facial body parts on slips of paper and put them in a paper bag. As you pull each slip of paper from the bag, point to that facial feature.

What other words and phrases do you need? Write or draw them on the face below.

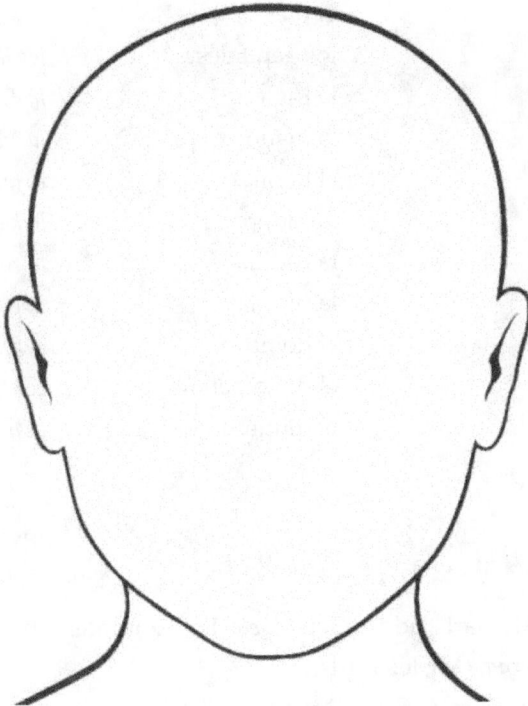

Parts of the Body - Body

Does your ... hurt?	¿Le duele(n)...?	*lay DWAY-lay(n)...*
Yes, my .... hurts.	Sí, me duele(n)....	*see may DWAY-lay(n)...*
No, my ... doesn't hurt.	No, no me duele(n)...	*no no may DWAY-lay(n)...*
ankle	el tobillo	*el toh-BEE-yoh*
arm	el brazo	*el BRAH-zoh*
back	la espalda	*la ay-SPAHL-dah*
behind/bottom	el trasero	*el trah-SAIR-oh*
breasts	los senos/las mamas	*los SAY-nohs/las MAH-mahs*
buttocks	los glúteos	*los GLOO-tay-ohs*
chest	el pecho	*el PAY-choh*
elbow	el codo	*el KOH-doh*
finger	el dedo	*el DAY-doh*
foot	el pie	*el PEE-ay*
genitals	los genitales	*los hay-nay-TAH-lays*
groin	la ingle	*la-EEN-glay*
hand	la mano	*la MAH-noh*
heel	el talón	*el tah-LONE*
hip	la cadera	*la kah-DARE-ah*
knee	la rodilla	*la roh-DEE-yah*
leg	la pierna	*la pee-AIR-nah*
shoulder	el hombro	*el OME-broh*
toe	el dedo del pie	*el DAY-doh dale pee-AY*
wrist	la muñeca	*la moo-NYAY-kah*

Grammar Note

For plural body parts, add an *n* to *duele*. For example:
Me duele la pierna. (My leg hurts.)
Me duelen las piernas. (My legs hurt.)

Conversation Activities: Parts of the Body - Body

Play "Simon Says": Play *Simon Dice* (pronounced see-MOAN DEE-say) to practice body parts. Some useful words include *toque* ("touch"- pronounced TOH-kay) and *levante* ("raise"- pronounced lay-VAHN-tay) For example, you can say, *Toque el estómogo* ("Touch your stomach") or *Levante la mano* ("Raise your hand").

What other words and phrases do you need? Write or draw them on the body below.

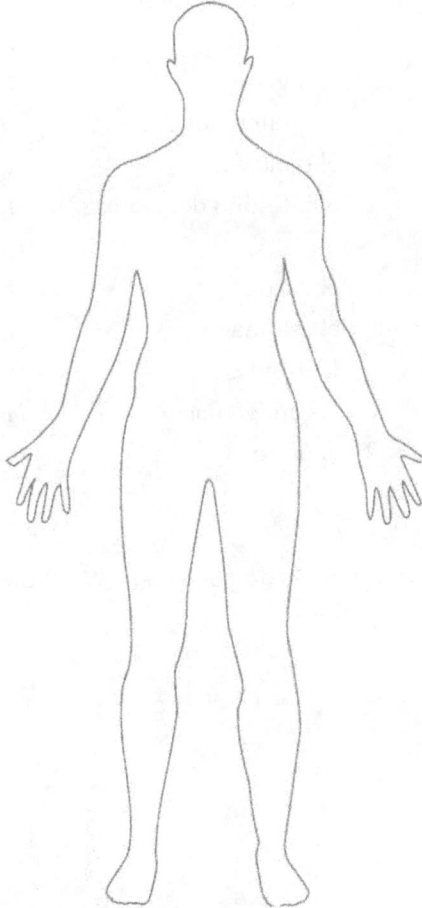

Organs

appendix	el apéndice	*el ah-PAIN-dee-say*
bladder	la vejiga	*la bay-HE-gah*
brain	el cerebro	*el sair-AY-broh*
colon	el colón	*el koh-LONE*
esophagus	el esófago	*el ay-SO-fah-goh*
gallbladder	la vesícula	*la bay-SEE-koo-lah*
heart	el corazón	*el core-ah-ZONE*
kidney	el riñón	*el reen-YONE*
large intestine	el intestino grueso	*el een-tay-STEEN-oh GRWAY-soh*
liver	el hígado	*el EE-gah-doh*
lungs	los pulmones	*los pool-MOH-nays*
pancreas	el páncreas	*el PAHN-kray-ahs*
small intestine	el intestino delgado	*el een-tay-STEEN-oh dale-GAH-doh*
spleen	el bazo	*el BAH-soh*
stomach	el estómago	*el ay-STOH-mah-goh*
thyroid gland	la tiroides	*la teer-oh-EE-days*
tonsils	las amígdalas	*las ah-MEEG-dah-lahs*
uterus	el útero	*el OO-tare-oh*

What other words and phrases do you need? Write them below.

Conversation Activities: Organs

Think back to your anatomy class. Draw and label the organs that you need to know for your job or are causing the most difficulty for you to remember.

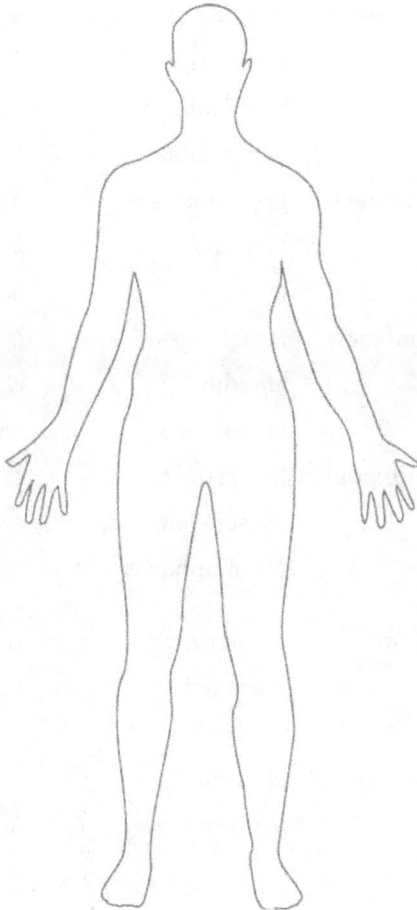

Bones

bone	el hueso	*el WAY-soh*
carpals (wrist)	las cárpales	*las KAR-pah-lays*
clavicle (collar bone)	la clavícula	*la klah-BEE-koo-lah*
cranium (skull)	el cráneo	*el KRAH-nee-oh*
elbow	el codo	*el KOH-doh*
femur (thighbone)	el fémur	*el FAY-moor*
fibula (lower leg bone)	la fíbula	*la FEE-boo-lah*
humerus (upper arm)	el húmero	*el OO-mare-oh*
joint	la articulación	*ar-tee-koo-lah-see-OWN*
mandible (jaw)	la mandíbula	*la mahn-DEE-boo-lah*
metatarsals (foot bones)	los metatarsos	*los may-tah-TAR-sohs*
patella (knee cap)	la rótula	*la ROH-too-lah*
pelvis	la pelvis	*la PALE-bees*
phalanges (fingers/ toes)	las falanges	*las fah-LAHN-hays*
radius (forearm)	el radio	*el RAH-dee-oh*
ribs	las costillas	*las koh-STEE-yahs*
scapula (shoulder blade)	la escápula	*la ay-SKAH-poo-lah*
skeleton	el esqueleto	*el ay-skay-LAY-toh*
spine	la columna vertebral	*la cole-OOM-nah bare-tay-BRAHL*
sternum (breast bone)	el esternón	*el ay-stairn-OWN*
tarsals (ankles)	los tarsos	*los TAR-sohs*
tibia (shin bone)	la tibia	*la TEE-bee-ah*
ulna (forearm)	el cúbito	*el KOO-bee-toh*
vertebrae	las vertebras	*las bare-TAY-brahs*

Conversation Activities: Bones

Label the bones that you need to know for your job or are causing the most difficulty for you to remember. (Note that the technical name is given for the bones, in which your patients may or may not be familiar.)

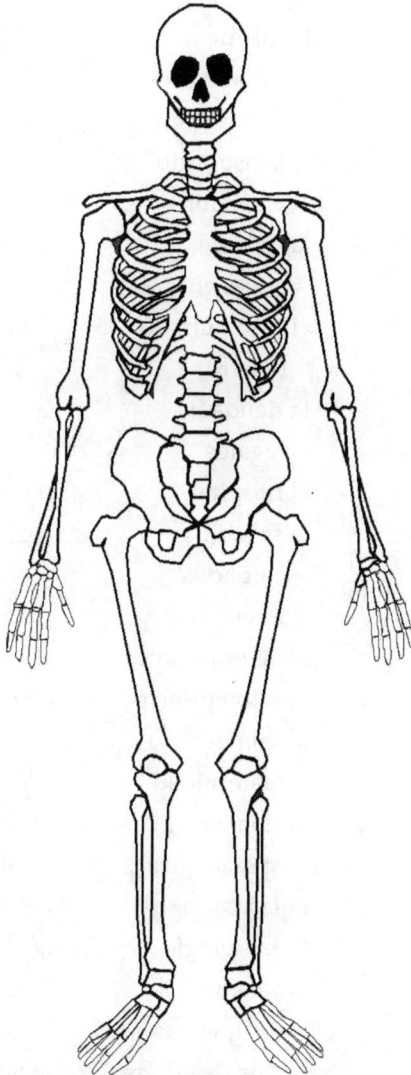

Places

Where is (the)...	¿Dónde está...?	*DOAN-day ay-STAH*
We are going to (the)...	Vamos a...	*BAH-mohs ah*
cafeteria	la cafetería	*la kah-fay-tare-EE-ah*
chapel	la capilla	*la kah-PEE-yah*
clinic	la clínica	*la KLEEN-ee-kah*
conference room	la sala de conferencias	*la SAH-lah day cone-fare-EHN-see-ahs*
delivery room	la sala de partos	*la SAH-lah day PAR-tohs*
doctor's office	el consultorio	*el cone-sool-TORE-ee-oh*
elevator	el elevador	*el ale-ay-bah-DOOR*
emergency room	la sala de emergencia	*la SAH-lah day ay-mare-HEHN-see-ah*
floor # (4)	el piso número (cuatro)	*el PEE-soh NOO-mare-oh (KWAH-troh)*
gift shop	la tienda de regalos	*la tee-AIN-dah day ray-GAH-los*
hospital	el hospital	*el oh-spee-TAHL*
intensive care	la sala de cuidados intensivos	*la SAH-lah day KWEE-dah-dohs een-tain-SEE-bohs*
laboratory	el laboratorio	*el lah-bore-ah-TORE-ee-oh*
main lobby	el salón principal	*el sah-LONE preen-see-PAHL*
maternity ward	la sala de maternidad	*la SAH-lah day mah-tare-nee-DAHD*
operating room	la sala de operaciones	*la SAH-lah day oh-pair-ah-see-OWN-ays*
pharmacy	la farmacia	*la farm-AH-see-ah*
radiology	la radiología	*la rah-dee-oh-low-HE-ah*
recovery room	la sala de recuperación	*la SAH-lah day ray-koo-pair-ah-see-OWN*
waiting room	la sala de espera	*la SAH-lah day ay-SPARE-ah*

Conversation Activities: Places

Incorporate both the Directions and Places. Choose a starting location and a "place" where you want to go. Give directions how to get there.

Play a word association game. One person says a common store or place in your area and the others say the Spanish word for this place. For example: One person says, "*St. John's*" and the other responds, "*iglesia*".

Large Group Activity: Using all of the Spanish vocabulary that you know (and some *Spanglish*), describe one of these places and have your partner/group guess what it is. If you prefer, play Charades to see if your partner/group can come up with the Spanish word.

Grammar Tip

Note the expression *Vamos al/ la...* on the previous page. *Vamos a...* means *We are going to...* If the word *a* comes into contact with the word *el*, a Spanish contraction is formed to become *al.* Therefore, *a + el = al.*

Examples:
Vamos *al* consultorio. (Vamos *a + el* banco.)
Vamos a la cafeteria.

Registration – Patient Data

What is your...?	¿Cuál es su...?	kwahl ace soo ___
name	nombre	NOME-bray
maiden name	nombre de soltera	NOME-bray day sole-TARE-ah
address	dirección	dee-rake-see-OWN
city	ciudad	see-oo-DAHD
state	estado	ay-STAH-doh
ZIP code	zona postal	SO-nah poh-STAHL
telephone #	número de teléfono	NOO-mare-oh day tay-LAY-foh-no
cell phone #	número de celular	NOO-mare-oh day say-loo-LAR
email address	dirección de correo electrónico	dee-rake-see-OWN day core-AY-oh ay-lake-TRAHN-ee-koh
date of birth	fecha de nacimiento	FAY-chah day nah-see-mee-EN-toh
age	edad	ay-DAHD
place of birth	lugar de nacimiento	loo-GAR day nah-see-mee-EN-toh
nationality	nacionalidad	nah-see-oh-nahl-ee-DAHD
sex	sexo	SEX-oh
social security number	número de seguro social	NOO-mare-oh day say-GOO-row so-see-AHL
first language	primer lenguaje	pree-MARE lang-GWAH-hay
height	altura	all-TOO-rah
weight	peso	PAY-so
marital status	estado civil	es-TAH-doh see-BEEL
place of employment	lugar de empleo	loo-GAR de aim-PLAY-oh
race	raza	RAH-sah

Registration – Phrases

Can I help you?	¿Le puedo ayudar?	*lay PWAY-doh ah-you-DAR*
You can wait over there.	Puede esperar allá.	*PWAY-day ay-spare-AR ah-YAH*
I will be right with you.	Enseguida le atiendo.	*ain-say-GEE-dah lay ah-tee-AIN-doh*
Wait in the room.	Espere en el consultorio.	*ay-SPARE-ay en el cone-sool-TORE-ee-oh*
Come.	Venga.	*BANE-gah*
Go with the nurse.	Vaya con la enfermera.	*BYE-ah cone la ain-fair-MARE-ah*
Take a seat please.	Tome asiento, por favor.	*TOH-may ah-see-AIN-toh pore fah-BORE*
Please fill out this paper.	Por favor, llene este papel.	*pore fah-BORE YAY-nay AY-stay pah-PALE*

Registration – Questions

Do you have...?	¿Tiene...?	*tee-AY-nay...*
an appointment	una cita	*OO-nah SEE-tah*
a family doctor	un médico general	*oon MAY-dee-koh hay-nare-AHL*
health insurance	seguro médico	*say-GOO-roh MAY-dee-koh*
your insurance card	su tarjeta de seguro	*soo tar-HAY-tah day say-GOO-roh*
the forms	los formularios	*los for-moo-LAR-ee-ohs*
identification	identificación	*ee-dane-tee-fee-kah-see-OWN*
Do you need...?	¿Necesita...?	*nay-say-SEE-tah*
a consultation	una consulta	*OO-nah cone-SOOL-tah*
a counselor	un consejero	*oon cone-say-HAIR-oh*
a follow-up appointment	una cita de seguimiento	*OO-nah SEE-tah day say-gee-mee-AIN-toh*
a wheelchair	una silla de ruedas	*OO-nah SEE-yah day roo-AY-dahs*
an exam	un examen	*oon ex-AH-mane*
an interpreter	un intérprete	*oon een-TARE-pray-tay*
to make a payment	hacer un pago	*ah-SARE oon PAH-goh*
to see the doctor	ver al médico	*bare ahl MAY-dee-koh*
Do you want...?	¿Quiere...?	*key-AIR-ay*
a sticker	una calcomanía	*OO-nah kahl-koh-mah-NEE-ah*
a piece of candy	un dulce	*oon DOOL-say*
a toy	un juguete	*oon hoo-GAY-tay*

Conversation Activities: Registration

Role-Play: Think about what happens when a patient walks into your medical facility. What happens? Who greets this person? What is asked of the patient? Use the previous "Registration" vocabulary to guide your role-play.

What other words and phrases do you need? Write them below.

Insurance

health insurance	el seguro médico	*el say-GOO-roh MAY-dee-koh*
benefits	los beneficios	*los bane-ay-FEE-see-ohs*
cost	el costo	*el KOH-stoh*
deductible	el deducible	*el day-doo-SEE-blay*
discount	el descuento	*el day-SKWEN-toh*
expenses	los gastos	*los GAH-stohs*
group	el grupo	*el GROO-poh*
member	el miembro	*el mee-AIM-broh*
plan	el plan	*el plahn*

Do you have health insurance?	¿Tiene seguro médico?	*tee-AIN-ay say-GOO-roh MAY-dee-koh*
What is your…?	¿Cuál es su…?	*kwahl es soo*
insurance company	compañía de seguros	*comb-pah-NYEE-ah*
primary insurance	seguro primario	*ay-GOO-roh pree-MAR-ee-ohs*
policy & group number	número de póliza y grupo	*NEW-mare-oh day POH-lee-sah ee GROO-poh*
member ID number	número de identificación de miembro	*NOO-mare-oh day ee-dane-tee-fee-kah-see-OWN day mee-AME-broh*
claim number	número de reclamación	*NOO-mare-oh day ray-klah-mah-see-OWN*
Is this self-pay?	¿Es costo a su cargo?	*ase KOH-stoh ah soo KAR-goh*
Your co-pay is…	Su co-pago es…	*soo koh-PAH-goh ase*
The effective date is…	La fecha de entrada en vigencia es…	*la FAY-chah day ain-TRAH-dah ain bee-HANE-see-ah ase*

Conversation Activities: Insurance

Role-Play: How does your medical facility deal with insurance and the various insurance companies? Think about who asks these questions and what they would ask. Use the previous "Insurance" vocabulary to guide your role-play.

What other words and phrases do you need? Write them below.

Medical History

Do you smoke?	¿Fuma?	*FOO-mah*
Do you drink alcohol?	¿Toma alcohol?	*TOH-mah al-koh-HOLE*
Do you use drugs?	¿Usa drogas?	*OO-sah DROH-gahs*
Do you have...?	¿Tiene...?	*tee-AIN-ay*
Have you had...?	¿Ha tenido?	*ah tay-NEE-doh*
AIDS	SIDA	*SEE-dah*
anemia	anemia	*ah-NAY-mee-ah*
asthma	asma	*AH-smah*
cancer	cáncer	*KAHN-sair*
chicken pox	varicela	*bah-ree-SAY-lah*
cholera	cólera	*KOH-lair-ah*
diabetes	diabetes	*dee-ah-BAY-tays*
diphtheria	difteria	*deef-TARE-ee-ah*
epilepsy	epilepsia	*ay-pee-LAPE-see-ah*
German measles	rubéola	*roo-BAY-oh-lah*
HIV	VIH	*bay ee AH-chay*
heart disease	enfermedad del corazón	*ain-fair-may-DAHD del core-ah-ZONE*
hepatitis	hepatitis	*ay-pah-TEE-tees*
leukemia	leucemia	*lay-oo-SAY-mee-ah*
measles	sarampión	*sar-ahm-pee-OWN*
meningitis	meningitis	*mane-een-HEE-tees*
mumps	paperas	*pah-PAIR-ahs*
pneumonia	pulmonía	*pool-moh-NEE-ah*
polio	polio	*POH-lee-oh*
rheumatic fever	fiebre reumática	*fee-AY-bray ray-oo-MAH-tee-kah*
tetanus	tétano	*TAY-tah-no*
tuberculosis	tuberculosis	*too-bare-koo-LOH-sees*
whooping cough	tos ferina/ convulsiva	*tohs fare-EE-nah/cone-bool-SEE-bah*

Conversation Activities: Medical History

Role-Play: Who takes your medical history? Do the patients fill out a form? Does someone verify the information from this form? Is this form translated into Spanish? Use the previous "Medical History" vocabulary to practice your pronunciation of the various conditions and diseases and to guide your role-play. Other useful phrases include *¿Hace cuánto?* (How long ago?) or *¿Cuándo?* (When).

What other words and phrases do you need? Write them below.

Common Symptoms

Are you sick?	¿Está enfermo/a?	*ay-STAH ain-FARE-moh/mah*
Do you have…?	¿Tiene…?	*tee-AIN-ay*
Have you had..?	¿Ha tenido…?	*ah tay-NEE-doh*
back pain	dolor de espalda	*doh-LORE day ay-SPAHL-dah*
bleeding	sangrado	*sahn-GRAH-doh*
chest pain	dolor en el pecho	*doh-LORE en el PAY-choh*
a cough	una tos	*OO-nah*
congestion	congestión	*cone-hay-stee-OWN*
constipation	estreñimiento	*ay-strain-yee-mee-AIN-toh*
a cough	un tos	*oon tohs*
diarrhea	diarrea	*dee-ah-RAY-ah*
dizziness	mareos	*mah-RAY-ohs*
an earache	un dolor de oído	*oon doh-LORE day oh-EE-doh*
a fever	una fiebre	*OO-nah fee-AY-bray*
a headache	un dolor de cabeza	*oon doh-LORE day kah-BAY-sah*
heartburn	acidez	*ah-see-DAYS*
high blood pressure	presión arterial alta	*pray-see-OWN ar-tare-ee-AHL AHL-tah*
hives	ronchas	*ROAN-chahs*
hoarseness	ronquera	*roan-KARE-ah*
itching	picazón	*pee-kah-ZONE*
pain	dolor	*doh-LORE*
a sore throat	un dolor de la garganta	*oon doh-LORE day la gar-GAHN-tah*
stomach pain	dolor de estómago	*doh-LORE day ay-STOH-mah-goh*
trouble breathing	dificultad de respirar	*dee-fee-cool-TAHD day ray-speer-AR*

Conversation Activities: Common Symptoms

Role-Play: These questions could be asked by a number of medical professionals. Create a role play scenario that makes the most sense in your medical facility. Act out a ridiculous scenario to keep it fun!

What other words and phrases do you need? Write them below.

Common Conditions and Injuries

What happened?	¿Qué pasó?	*kay pah-SOH*
You have…	Tiene …	*tee-AY-nay*
You have had…	Ha tenido…	*ah tay-NEE-doh*
a cold	un resfriado	*oon ray-sfree-AH-doh*
a virus	un virus	*oon BEE-roos*
the flu	la gripe	*la GREE-pay*
a bad cut	una cortada seria	*OO-nah kor-TAH-dah SAIR-ee-ah*
a bad fall	una caída grave	*OO-nah kie-EE-dah GRAH-bay*
breathing difficulties	dificultad al respirar	*deef-ee-cool-TAHD ahl ray-speer-AR*
a broken arm	un brazo roto	*oon BRAH-zoh ROH-toh*
a broken leg	una pierna rota	*OO-nah pee-AIR-nah roh-tah*
dehydration	deshidratación	*days-hee-drah-tah-see-OWN*
a (head) wound	una herida (en la cabeza)	*OO-nah air-EE-dah (en la kah-BAY-sah*
a heart attack	un ataque al corazón	*oon ah-TAH-kay ahl core-ah-ZONE*
a seizure	un ataque	*oon ah-TAH-kay*
a sprained ankle	una torcedura de tobillo	*OO-nah tore-say-DO-rah day toh-BEE-yoh*
a stroke	un derrame cerebral	*oon day-RAH-may sair-ay-BRAHL*

Conversation Activities: Common Conditions and Injuries

Role-Play: After asking the patient several questions and learning about symptoms, create various role-plays where you can use as many of these conditions and injuries as possible.

What other words and phrases do you need? Write them below.

Emergencies

What happened?	¿Qué pasó?	*kay pah-SO*
Are you hurt?	¿Está herido?	*ay-STAH air-EE-doh*
Are you in pain?	¿Le duele?	*lay DWELL-lay*
Can you move?	¿Puede moverse?	*PWAY-day moe-BARE-say*
Do you need an ambulance?	¿Necesita una ambulancia?	*nay-say-SEE-tah OO-nah ahm-boo-LAHN-see-ah*
Call an ambulance!	¡Llame una ambulancia!	*YAH-may OO-nah ahm-boo-LAHN-see-ah*
Call 911!	¡Llame al nueve uno uno!	*YAH-may ahl NWAY-bay OON-oh OON-oh*
Call his/her family!	¡Llame a su familia!	*YAH-may ah soo fah-MEE-lee-ah*
Calm down.	Cálmese.	*CAHL-may-say*
Don't move.	No se mueva.	*no say MWAY-bah*
We are looking for help.	Estamos buscando ayuda.	*ay-STAH-mohs boos-KAHN-doh ah-YOO-dah*

Conversation Activities: Emergencies

Role-Play: Perhaps you come upon an accident outside of your medical facility. Create a role-play scenario where it would make sense to use some of these phrases.

What other words and phrases do you need? Write them below.

Actions and Commands

bend down	agáchese	*ah-GACH-ay-say*
breathe (deeply)	respire (profundo)	*ray-SPEER-ay pro-FOON-doh*
bring	traiga	*TRY-gah*
call	llame	*YAH-may*
calm down	cálmese	*KAHL-may-say*
carry	lleve	*YAY-bay*
come closer	acérquese	*ah-SARE-kay-say*
do this	haga esto	*AH-gah AY-stoh*
extend	extienda	*ayks-TEE-ain-dah*
follow	siga	*SEE-gah*
get undressed	desvístase	*days-BEE-stah-say*
get up	súbase	*SOO-bah-say*
go	vaya	*BAH-yah*
go down	baje	*BAH-hay*
go up	suba	*SOO-bah*
grab	agarre	*ah-GAH-ray*
hold	mantenga	*mahn-TAIN-gah*
hurry up	apúrese	*ah-POO-ray-say*
join, put together	junte	*HOON-tay*
lean	inclínese	*een-KLEEN-ay-say*
let go	suéltese	*SWALE-tay-say*
lie down	acuéstese	*ah-KWAY-stay-say*
lower	baje	*BAH-hay*
move	muévase	*MWAY-bah-say*
open (your mouth)	abra (la boca)	*AH-brah (la BOH-kah)*
point (to)	señale (a)	*sane-YAH-lay*
pull	jale	*HAH-lay*
push	empuje	*aim-POO-hay*
put	ponga	*PONE-gah*
put on	póngase	*PONE-gah-say*
raise	levante	*lay-BAHN-tay*

reach	estire	*ay-STEER-ay*
relax	relaje	*ray-LAH-hay*
rest	descanse	*day-SKAHN-say*
say "ah"	diga "ah"	*DEE-gah ah*
separate	separe	*say-PARE-ay*
show me	muéstreme	*MWAY-stray-may*
sign	firme	*FEER-may*
sit down	siéntese	*see-AIN-tay-say*
squeeze	apriete	*ah-pree-AY-tay*
stand up	levántese	*lay-BAHN-tay-say*
stick out your tongue	saque la lengua	*SAH-kay la LANG-gwah*
straighten	enderece	*ain-dare-AY-say*
stretch	estírese	*ay-STEER-aysay*
support	apoye	*ah-POY-ay*
take	tome	*TOH-may*
take off	quítese	*KEE-tay-say*
tell me	avíseme	*ah-BEE-say-may*
touch	toque	*TOH-kay*
try	trate	*TRAH-tay*
turn around	voltéese	*bowl-TAY-ay-say*
turn over	dése la vuelta	*DAY-say la BWELL-tah*
undress	desvístase	*day-SBEE-stay-say*
wait	espérese	*ay-SPARE-ay-say*
wake up	despiértese	*day-spee-AIR-tay-say*

Note that the above "commands" are in the *usted*, or formal, conjugation.

Conversation Activities: Actions and Commands

What is missing in this list of commands that you use on a daily basis?

Go to on online dictionary (such as www.WordReference.com) to first look the word up, then to an online Spanish verb conjugator (such as http://www.spanishdict.com/conjugation) to see how you could say it politely, yet as a command. (You will be looking for the formal *usted* "command" or "imperative" form, generally located on the bottom of the page.)

Use this space to write down additional "commands" you use in your job.

Pain - Descriptions

Are you in pain?	¿Le duele?	*lay DWAY-lay*
Are you in a lot of pain?	¿Le duele mucho?	*lay DWAY-lay MOO-choh*
What hurts?	¿Qué le duele?	*kay lay DWAY-lay*
Where does it hurt?	¿Dónde le duele?	*DOAN-day lay DWAY-lay*
It hurts here.	Me duele aquí.	*may DWAY-lay ah-KEY*
Is your pain...?	¿Es su dolor...?	*ace soo doh-LORE*
burning	quemante	*kay-MAHN-tay*
constant	constante	*cone-STAHN-tay*
deep	profundo	*pro-FOON-doh*
dull	sordo	*SORE-doh*
intermittent	intermitente	*een-tare-mee-TAIN-tay*
mild	moderado	*mow-DARE-ah-doh*
severe	muy fuerte	*MOO-ee FWAIR-tay*
sharp	agudo	*ah-GOO-doh*
stable	estable	*ay-STAH-blay*
throbbing	pulsante	*pool-SAHN-tay*
worse	peor	*pay-ORE*
Rate your pain on a scale of 1 to 10 with 10 being the worst.	Califique su dolor en una escala del 1 al 10, siendo 10 el peor.	*kah-lee-FEE-kay soo doh-LORE ain OON-nah ay-SKAH-lah del OO-noh ahl dee-AYS, see-AIN-doh dee-AYS el pay-ORE*

Pain - Questions

What were you doing when this happened?	¿Qué estaba haciendo cuando pasó esto?	*kay ay-STAH-bah ah-see-AIN-doh KWAHN-doh pah-SOH AY-stoh*
Did it come on suddenly/slowly?	¿Comenzó de forma repentina/lenta?	*koh-mane-SOH day FOR-mah ray-pane-TEE-nah/LANE-tah*
What makes this condition better or worse?	¿Qué hace que esta condición sea mejor o peor?	*kay AH-say kay AY-stah cone-dee-see-OWN SAY-ah may-HORE oh pay-ORE*
Did this get better when you rested?	¿Mejoró cuando usted descansó?	*may-hore-OH KWAHN-doh oo-STADE day-skahn-SOH*
Did you take a medication?	¿Tomó alguna medicina?	*toh-MOH ahl-GOO-nah may-dee-SEE-nah*
Does the pain radiate?	¿El dolor se extiende?	*el doh-LORE say akes-tee-AIN-day*
Is it located in one specific area?	¿Está localizado en un área específica?	*ay-STAH loh-kah-lee-SAH-doh ain oon AH-ree-ah ay-spay-SEE-fee-kah*
How long has it been since the pain started?	¿Cuánto tiempo ha pasado desde que comenzó el dolor?	*KWAHN-toh tee-AIM-poh ah pah-SAH-doh DAY-sday kay koh-mane-SOH el doh-LORE*

Conversation Activities: Pain

Role-Play: Think of your job and the questions you need to ask regarding a patient's pain. Create a role-play scenario between a patient and a medical professional that makes sense for job.

What other words and phrases do you need? Write them below.

Care

I'm going to...	Voy a...	*boy ah*
draw blood	sacar sangre	*sah-KAR SAHN-gray*
listen to your lungs	auscultarle	*ow-skool-TAR-lay*
measure your blood pressure	medirle la presión	*may-DEER-lay la pray-see-OWN*
measure your vital signs	medir su signos vitales	*may-DEER soos SEEG-nohs bee-TAH-lays*
take your height and weight	medirle y pesarle	*may-DEER-lay ee pay-SAR-lay*
take your pulse	tomarle el pulso	*toh-MAR-lay el POOL-soh*
take your temperature	tomarle la temperatura	*toh-MAR-lay la tame-pare-ah-TOO-rah*

You need (a)...	Necesita...	*nay-say-SEE-tah*
bandage	un vendaje	*oon bain-DAH-hay*
cast	un yeso	*oon YAY-soh*
operation	una operación	*OO-nah oh-pare-ah-see-OWN*
shot	una inyección	*OO-nah een-yek-see-OWN*
sling	un cabestrillo	*oon kah-bay-STREE-yoh*
stitches	unas puntadas	*OO-nahs poon-TAH-dahs*

I need a...	Necesito...	*nay-say-SEE-tah*
blood sample	una muestra de sangre	*OO-nah moo-AY-strah day SAHN-gray*
count	un recuento	*oon ray-KWAIN-toh*
stool sample	una muestra de excremento	*OO-nah moo-AY-strah day ex-cray-MAIN-toh*
urine sample	una muestra de orina	*OO-nah moo-AY-strah day or-EE-nah*
x-ray	una radiografía	*OO-nah rah-dee-oh-grah-FEE-a*

Conversation Activities: Care

Think about your role and what you often say to your patients that you are going to "do" to them or that they "need". What else do you "need" from them? Write these words and phrases below.

Discharge

You have to...	Tiene que...	*tee-AY-nay kay*
bathe	bañarse	*bahn-YAR-say*
gargle	hacer gárgaras	*ah-SAIR GAR-gar-ahs*
wash	lavarse	*lah-BAR-say*

You should...	Debería...	*day-bare-EE-ah*
be active	ser activo	*sare ahk-TEE-boh*
maintain a healthy weight	mantener un peso saludable	*mahn-tay-NARE oon PAY-soh sahl-oo-DAH-blay*
reduce stress	reducir estrés	*ray-doo-SEER ay-STRACE*
limit alcohol	limitar el alcohol	*lee-mee-TAR el ahl-koh-OHL*
quit smoking	dejar de fumar	*day-HAR day foo-MAR*
eat more vegetables and fruit	comer más verduras y frutas	*koh-MARE mahs bare-DOO-rahs ee FROO-tahs*
drink more water	tomar más agua	*toh-MAR mahs AH-gwah*
limit sugary drinks	limitar bebidas azucaradas	*lee-mee-TAR bay-BEE-dahs ah-soo-kar-AH-dahs*

<u>Diet</u>

In the first few seeks/days, eat/drink a diet of...	En las primeras semanas/días, tome una dieta de...	*ain las pree-MARE-ahs say-MAH-nahs/DEE-ahs, TOH-may OO-nah dee-AY-tah day*
In the following weeks, eat/drink a diet of...	En las siguientes semanas, tome una dieta de...	*en las see-gee-AIN-tays say-MAH-nahs TOH-may OO-nah dee-AY-tah day*

Discharge - Instructions

Wound Care

You can bathe in (3) days.	Se puede bañar en (3) días.	*say PWAY-day bahn-YAR en (trace) DEE-ahs*
Leave your bandage on until your scheduled appointment.	Deje el vendaje hasta su cita programada.	*DAY-hay el bane-DAH-hay AH-stah soo SEE-tah pro-grah-MAH-dah*
Remove your bandage in (3) hours.	Quite el vendaje en (3) horas.	*KEE-tay el bain-DAH-hay en (trace) ORE-ahs*

Activity

Do not attend work/school for (5) days.	No puede asistir al trabajo/la escuela por (5) días	*no PWAY-day ah-see-STEER ahl trah-BAH-hoh/la ay-SKAY-lah pore (SEEN-koh) DEE-ahs*
Do not play contact sports for (8) weeks.	No puede hacer deportes de contacto físico por (8) semanas	*no PWAY-day ah-SARE day-PORE-tays day cone-TAHK-toh FEE-see-kah pore (OH-choh) say-MAH-nahs*
Do not swim in the pool for (3) weeks.	No puede nadar en la piscina por (3) semanas.	*no PWAY-day nah-DAR en la pee-SEE-nah pore (trace) say-MAH-nahs*
Do not lift more than (10) pounds.	No levante más de (10) libras.	*no lay-BAHN-tay mahs day (dee-ACE) LEE-brahs*
You will be given an appointment for a follow-up.	Se le dará una cita para una consulta de seguimiento.	*say lay dar-AH OO-nah SEE-tah PAH-rah OO-nah cone-SOOL-tah day say-gee-mee-AIN-toh*
If you have questions or problems, call...	Si tiene preguntas o problemas, llame al...	*see tee-AIN-ay pray-GOON-tahs o prohhh-BLAME-ahs YAH-may ahl*

Conversation Activities: Discharge

Role-Play: Think about your specialty. What else do you say to patients when they are leaving your medical facility and/or a particular treatment?

What other words and phrases do you need? Write them below.

Section 3: Specialty Spanish

Are you still looking for more specific vocabulary? This section is going to be a bit different because I am not going to give you any conversation or role-play activities. By now, you have an idea of how you can practice these words with a co-worker, family member, or friend. Instead, what I am giving you is a list of common vocabulary words and phrases. Do not focus on memorizing everything here. Just get out a highlighter and highlight what you actually use daily in your job. What is not there, I have left space for you to write down your own words and phrases that you need for your job.

For words, as you have seen me recommend throughout the book, I will again recommend www.WordReference.com. What makes this online dictionary different from the others is the section way down at the bottom where people ask their questions on how to say words and phrases in Spanish. Native speakers from all over the world then answer how they would say something in their region or dialect. It even has an audio tool where you can hear how a word is pronounced. This is a great learning tool! You can also look them in the comprehensive medical Spanish dictionary, such as, *Medical Dictionary/Diccionario Médico* by Glenn T. Rogers, MD, for very specific medical vocabulary in Spanish.

For phrases that you need to learn how to say, I "cautiously" recommend Google Translate (translate.google.com). I cannot emphasize enough, however, how careful you must be using this tool. While the translations are steadily improving with the technological advances, it is still a machine translation. Before you start memorizing many phrases from Google Translate, try to find a native Spanish-speaker to see if he/she would approve of the phrase or if there is a better way to say it.

Allergies & Asthma

Is he/she allergic to…?	¿Es alérgico/a a…?	ase ah-LARE-hee-koh/ah ah
animal dander	la caspa animal	la KAH-spah ah-nee-MAHL
aspirin	la aspirina	la ah-speer-EE-nah
bees	las abejas	las ah-BAY-hahs
cats	los gatos	los GAH-tohs
dairy products	los productos lácteos	los pro-DOOK-tohs LAHK-tay-ohs
dogs	los perros	los PAY-rohs
dust mites	los ácaros	los AH-kar-ohs
eggs	los huevos	los HWAY-bohs
flour	la harina	la ah-REE-nah
gluten	el gluten	el GLOO-tane
latex	el látex	el LAH-takes
milk	la leche	la LAY-chay
mold	el moho	el MOH-oh
peanuts	los cacahuates	los kah-kah-WAH-tays
penicillin	la penicilina	la pay-nee-see-LEE-nah
pollen	el polen	el POH-lane
shellfish	los mariscos	los mah-REE-skohs
soy	la soya	la SOY-yah
tree nuts	los nueces de árbol	los NWAY-says day AR-bohl
wheat	el trigo	el TREE-goh

Additional Words and Phrases:

Allergies & Asthma

What are your symptoms?	¿Cuáles son sus síntomas?	*KWAHL-ays sown soos SEEN-toh-mahs*
Do you have…?	¿Tiene…?	*tee-AY-nay…*
itching	comezón/picazón	*koh-may-ZONE/pee-kah-ZONE*
swelling	hinchazón	*een-chah-ZONE*
hives	urticaria	*oor-tee-KAR-ee-ah*
sneezing	estornudos	*ay-stor-NOO-dohs*
difficulty breathing	dificultad para respirar	*dee-fee-kool-TAHD PAH-rah ray-speer-AR*
a running nose	secreción nasal	*say-kray-see-OWN nah-SAHL*
eczema	eczema	*ayks-SAY-mah*

Additional Words and Phrases:

Cardiology Vocabulary

aorta	la aorta	*la ah-ORE-tah*
artery	la arteria	*la ar-TARE-ee-ah*
atrium	la aurícula	*la ow-REE-koo-lah*
septum	el tabique	*el tah-BEE-kay*
valve	la válvula	*la BAHL-boo-lah*
blood vessel	el vaso sanguíneo	*el BAH-soh sahn-GEE-nay-oh*
vein	la vena	*la BANE-ah*
ventricle	el ventrículo	*el bane-TREE-koo-lah*
heartbeat	el ritmo cardíaco	*el REET-moh kar-DEE-ah-koh*
You have (a/an)…	Tiene…	*tee-AY-nay*
You have had (a/an)…	Ha tenido…	*ah tay-NEE-doh*
aneurysm	una aneurisma	*OO-nah ahn-yare-EES-mah*
arrhythmia	una arritmia	*OO-nah ah-REET-mee-ah*
blocked artery	una arteria obstruida	*OO-nah ar-TARE-ee-ah ohb-stroo-EE-dah*
blood clot	un coágulo sanguíneo	*oon KWAH-goo-loh sahn-GEE-nay-oh*
heart attack	un ataque al corazón	*oon ah-TAH-kay ahl kore-ah-ZONE*
strained muscle	un músculo forzado	*oon MOO-skoo-loh fore-SAH-doh*
hardening (of the arteries)	endurecimiento (de las arterias)	*ain-doo-ray-see-mee-AIN-toh (day las ar-TARE-ee-ahs)*
atrial fibrillation	fibrilación atrial	*fee-bree-lah-see-OWN ah-tree-AHL*
ventricular fibrillation	fibrilación ventricular	*fee-bree-lah-see-OWN bane-tree-koo-LAR*
hypertension	hipertensión arterial	*ee-pare-tane-see-OWN ar-tare-ee-AHL*

Additional Words and Phrases:

Cardiology Questions

Do you have...?	¿Tiene...?	*tee-AY-nay*
burning	ardor	*ar-DORE*
chest pains	dolores en el pecho	*doh-LORE-ays ane el PAY-choh*
heart murmurs	soplo en el corazón	*SOH-ploh ane el kore-ah-ZONE*
irregular heartbeats	latidos de corazón irregulares	*lah-TEE-dohs day kore-ah-ZONE*
shortness of breath	falta de aliento	*FAHL-tah day ah-lee-ANE-toh*
a lot of perspiration	mucho sudor	*MOO-choh soo-DORE*
tingling	hormigueo	*ore-mee-GAY-oh*

Was it a sharp or dull pain?	¿Fue un dolor agudo o sordo?	*fway oon doh-LORE ah-GOO-doh oh SORE-doh*
How long ago?	¿Hace cuánto tiempo?	*AH-say KWAHN-toh tee-AME-poh*
How often?	¿Con qué frecuencia?	*cone kay fray-KWAIN-see-ah*

You need (a/an)...	Necesita...	*nay-say-SEE-tah*
angioplasty	una angioplastia	*OO-nah ahn-hee-oh-plah-STEE-ah*
anticoagulant	un anticoagulante	*oon ahn-tee-kwahl-goo-LAHN-tay*
bypass surgery	bypass coronario	*BYE-pahs kore-oh-NAR-ee-oh*
cardiac catheterization	cateterismo cardíaco	*kah-tay-tare-EES-moh kar-DEE-ah-koh*
electrocardiogram	un electrocardiograma	*oon ay-lake-troh-kar-dee-oh-GRAH-mah*
pacemaker	un marcapasos	*oon mar-kah-PAH-sohs*

Additional Words and Phrases:

Dentistry – General Vocabulary

cavity	la caries	*la KAR-ee-ays*
cleaning	la limpieza	*la leem-ee-AY-sah*
dental floss	el hilo dental	*el EE-loh DANE-tahl*
denture	la dentadura postiza	*la dane-tah-DOO-rah poh-STEE-sah*
filling	el empaste	*el ame-PAH-stay*
gums	las encías	*las ane-SEE-yahs*
molar	la muela	*la MWAY-lah*
plaque	la placa	*la PLAH-kah*
tartar	el sarro	*el SAH-roh*
tooth	el diente	*el dee-ANE-tay*
toothache	el dolor de muelas	*el doh-LORE day MWAY-lahs*
toothbrush	el cepillo de dientes	*el say-PEE-oh day dee-ANE-tays*
toothpaste	la pasta de dientes	*la PAH-stah day dee-ANE-tays*

Commands

bite	muerda	*MWAIR-dah*
brush	cepíllese	*say-PEE-yay-say*
gargle	haga gárgaras	*AH-gah GAR-gar-ahs*
chew	mastique	*mah-STEE-kay*
open your mouth	abra la boca	*AH-brah la BOH-kah*
rinse	enjuáguese	*ane-HWAH-gay-say*
spit	escupa	*ay-SKOO-pah*

Additional Words and Phrases:

Dentistry – Examination

Do you have problems with your...?	¿Tiene problemas con...?	*tee-AY-nay pro-BLAY-mahs cone*
baby tooth	el diente de leche	*el dee-ANE-tay day LAY-chay*
canine tooth	el colmillo	*el kohl-MEE-yoh*
jaw	la mandíbula	*la mahn-DEE-boo-lah*
palate	el paladar	*el pah-lah-DAR*
root	la raíz	*la rah-EESE*
wisdom tooth	la muela del juicio	*la MWAY-lah del HWEE-see-oh*
You have...	Tiene...	*tee-AY-nay*
a cavity	una caries	*OO-nah KAR-ee-ays*
a decayed tooth	un diente cariado	*oon dee-ANE-tay kar-ee-AH-doh*
a sore	una úlcera	*OO-nah OOL-sare-ah*
an abscess	un absceso	*oon ahb-SAY-soh*
an impaction	una impacción	*OO-nah eem-pahk-see-OWN*
an infection	una infección	*OO-nah een-fake-see-OWN*
bad breath	mal aliento	*mahl ah-lee-ANE-toh*
inflammation	inflamación	*een-flah-mah-see-OWN*
You need...	Necesita...	*nay-say-SEE-tah*
a crown	una corona	*OO-nah kore-OH-nah*
a root canal	una endodoncia	*OO-nah ane-do-DOHN-see-ah*
an extraction	una extracción	*OO-nah ayk-strahk-see-OWN*
anesthesia	anestesia	*ah-nay-STAY-see-ah*
braces	frenillos	*fray-NEE-yohs*
dental implants	implantes dentales	*eem-PLAHN-tays dane-TAH-lays*
X rays	rayos equis	*RAH-yohs AY-kees*

Additional Words and Phrases:

Geriatrics

Does he/she have…?	¿Tiene …?	tee-AY-nay
Has he/she had…?	¿Ha tenido…?	ah tay-NEE-doh
chronic fatigue	fatiga crónica	fah-TEE-gah KROH-nee-kah
cold or numb feet	pies fríos o entumidos	pee-AYS FREE-ohs oh ain-too-MEE-dohs
difficulty swallowing	dificultad para tragar	dee-fee-kool-TAHD PAH-rah trah-GAR
easy bruising	moretes fácilmente	more-AY-tays FAH-seel-main-tay
excessive mood swings	cambios de humor excesivo	KAHM-bee-ohs day oo-MORE ayk-say-SEE-boh
fainting	desmayos	days-MAH-yohs
gout	gota	GOH-tah
hand tremors	temblores de manos	tame-BLOR-ays day MAH-nohs
loss of appetite	perdida de apetito	pare-DEE-dahd day ah-pay-TEE-toh
memory loss	perdida de la memoria	pare-DEE-dah day la may-MORE-ee-ah
muscle weakness	debilidad muscular	day-bee-lee-DAHD moo-skoo-LAR
nervousness	nerviosismo	nare-bee-oh-SEE-smoh
numbness	entumecimiento	ain-too-may-see-mee-AIN-toh
swollen ankles	tobillos hinchados	toh-BEE-yohs een-CHAH-dohs
varicose veins	várices	BAR-ee-says
an advance directive	una directiva anticipada	OO-nah dee-rake-TEE-bah ahn-tee-see-PAH-dah
a living will	un testamento en vida	oon tay-stah-MAIN-toh ain BEE-dah
a healthcare proxy	un representante para la atención médica	oon ray-pray-sane-TAHN-tay PAH-rah la ah-tane-see-OWN MAY-dee-kah

Additional Words and Phrases:

Mental Health – Feelings

English	Spanish	Pronunciation
Are you...?	¿Está...?	*ay-STAH*
I am...	Estoy...	*ay-STOY*
Do you feel...?	¿Se siente...?	*say see-AIN-tay*
I feel...	Me siento...	*may see-AIN-toh*
afraid	asustado	*ah-soo-STAH-doh*
angry	enojado	*ain-oh-HAH-doh*
anxious	ansioso	*ahn-see-OH-soh*
ashamed	avergonzado	*ah-bare-gohn-SAH-doh*
bored	aburrido	*ah-boo-REE-doh*
calm	tranquilo	*trahn-KEEL-oh*
confused	confundido	*cone-foon-DEE-doh*
depressed	deprimido	*day-pree-MEE-doh*
embarrassed	apenado	*ah-pane-AH-doh*
frustrated	frustrado	*froo-STRAH-doh*
furious	furioso	*foo-ree-OH-soh*
guilty	culpable	*kool-PAH-blay*
happy	contento	*cone-TANE-toh*
impatient	impaciente	*eem-pah-see-AIN-tay*
nervous	nervioso	*nare-bee-OH-soh*
relieved	aliviado	*ah-lee-bee-AH-doh*
sad	triste	*TREE-stay*
sensitive	sensible	*sane-SEE-blay*
surprised	sorprendido	*sore-prane-DEE-doh*
tense	tenso	*TANE-soh*
tired	cansado	*kahn-SAH-doh*
uncomfortable	incómodo	*een-KOH-moh-doh*
unhappy	descontento	*days-cone-TANE-toh*
worried	preocupado	*pray-oh-koo-PAH-doh*

Grammar Note

Remember that adjectives that end in an *o* refer to males. Change the *o* to an *a* for females. For example: *Gerardo está content**o**. Susana está cansad**a**.*

Additional Words and Phrases:

Mental Health – Stress

In order to...	Para...	*PAH-rah...*
get better	mejorarse	*may-hore-AR-say*
manage your emotions	manejar las emociones	*mahn-ay-HAR las ay-moh see-OWN-ays*
relieve stress	aliviar el estrés	*ah-LEE-bee-ar el ay-STRASE*
resolve a problem	resolver un problema	*ray-sohl-BARE oon proh-BLAME-ah*
take things calmly	tomar las cosas con calma	*to-MAR las KOH-sahs cone KAHL-mah*
You have to...	Hay que...	*eye kay*
You should...	Debería...	*day-bay-REE-ah*
enjoy life	disfrutar la vida	*dees-froo-TAR la BEE-dah*
exercise	hacer ejercicio	*ah-SARE ay-hare-SEE-see-oh*
find a balance	encontrar un equilibrio	*ain-cone-TRAR oon ay-key-LEE-bree-oh*
get enthused about something	animarse	*ah-nee-MAR-say*
have good habits	tener buenos hábitos	*tay-NARE BWAY-nahs AH-bee-tohs*
laugh	reírse	*ray-EER-say*
maintain a balanced diet	mantener una dieta equilibrada	*mahn-tane-AIR OO-nah dee-AY-tah ay-kee-lee-BRAH-dah*
relax	relajarse	*ray-lah-HAR-say*
rest	descansar	*day-skahn-SAR*
sleep enough	dormir lo suficiente	*door-MEER loh soo-fee-see AIN-tay*
smile	sonreír	*sohn-ray-EER*
take care of yourself	cuidarse	*kwee-DAR-say*

Additional Words and Phrases:

Mental Health – Mental Illness

Do you suffer from...?	¿Padece de...?	*pah-DAY-say day*
Have you suffered from...?	¿Ha padecido de...?	*ah pah-day-SEE-doh day*
addiction	adicción	*ah-deek-see-OWN*
aggression	agresión	*ah-gray-see-OWN*
bipolar disorder	la enfermedad bipolar	*la ain-fare-mee-DAHD bee-pole-AR*
delirium	el delirio	*el day-LEE-ree-oh*
dementia	demencia	*day-MANE-see-ah*
dependence on substance	dependencia de una sustancia	*day-pane-DANE-see-ah day OO-nah soo-STAH-see-ah*
depression	la depresión	*la day-pray-see-OWN*
hallucinations	las alucinaciónes	*las ah-loo-see-nah-see-OWN-ays*
insomnia	el insomnio	*el een-SOHM-nee-oh*
mania	la manía	*la mah-NEE-ah*
panic attacks	ataques de pánico	*ah-TAH-kays day PAH-nee-koh*
paranoia	la paranoia	*la par-ah-NOY-ah*
phobias	las fobias	*las FOH-bee-ahs*
psychosis	la psicosis	*la see-KOH-sees*
schizophrenia	la esquizofrenia	*la ay-skee-soh-FRANE-ee-ah*
substance withdrawal	síntomas causados por la desintoxicación	*SEEN-toh-mahs cow-SAH-dohs pore la day-seen-toke-see-kah-see-OWN*

Additional Words and Phrases:

More Mental Health Issues

Do you have...	¿Tiene...?	*tee-AY-nay*
Have you had...	¿Ha tenido...?	*ah tay-NEE-doh*

...episodes	episodios de...	*ay-pee-SOH-dee-ohs day*
attention deficit disorder	síndrome de déficit atencial	*SEEN-droh-may day DAY-fee-seet ah-tane-see-AHL*
depressive	depresivo	*day-pray-SEE-boh*
hypomania	hipomanía	*ee-poh-mah-NEE-ah*
manic	manía	*mah-NEE-ah*
mood	estado de ánimo	*ay-STAH-doh day AH-nee-moh*

... disorder	trastorno de ...	*trah-STORE-noh day*
acute stress	estrés agudo	*ay-STRACE ah-GOO-doh*
communication	comunicación	*koh-moo-nee-kah-see-OWN*
eating	la alimentación	*la ah-lee-mane-tah-see-OWN*
learning	aprendizaje	*ah-prane-dee-SAH-hay*
obsessive compulsive	obsesivo compulsivo	*ohb-say-SEE-boh cohm-pool-SEE-boh*
panic	pánico	*PAH-nee-koh*
post-traumatic stress	estrés postraumático	*ay-STRACE poh-strauh-MAH-tee-koh*
trauma	trauma	*TRAUH-mah*

Additional Words and Phrases:

OB-GYN Vocabulary

abdomen	el abdomen, el vientre, la barriga	*el ahb-DOH-mane, el bee-ANE-tray, la bah-REE-gah*
abortion	el aborto provocado	*el ah-BORE-toh proh-boh-KAH-doh*
birth	el parto	*el PAR-toh*
breasts	los senos/las mamas	*los SAY-nohs/las MAH-mahs*
cervix	el cérvix, el cuello de matriz	*el SARE-beeks, el KWAY-yoh day mah-TREEZ*
Cesarean	la cesárea	*la say-SAR-ay-ah*
contraceptive	el anticonceptivo	*el ahn-tee-cone-sape-TEE-boh*
cramps	los cólicos, los dolores menstruales	*los KOH-lee-kohs, los doh-LORE-ays mane-stroo-AH-lays*
Fallopian tubes	las trompas/los tubos de Falopio	*las TROHM-pahs/los TOO-bohs day fah-LOH-pee-oh*
mammogram	el mamograma	*el mah-moh-GRAH-mah*
miscarriage	el aborto espontáneo	*el ah-BORE-toh ay-spone-TAH-nay-oh*
natural birth	el parto natural	*el PAR-toh nah-too-RAHL*
nipple	el pezón	*el pay-SONE*
ovary	el ovario	*el oh-BAR-ee-oh*
pap smear	el Papanicolaou	*el pah-pah-nee-kohl-OW*
period	la regla	*la RAY-glah*
pregnancy	el embarazo	*el ame-bar-AH-soh*
uterus	el útero/la matriz	*el OO-tare-oh/la mah-TREEZ*
vagina	la vagina	*la bah-HEE-nah*
to be pregnant	estar embarazada	*ay-STAR ame-bah-rah-SAH-dah*
to give birth	dar a luz	*dar ah loos*

Additional Words and Phrases:

OB/GYN - Questions

When was...?	¿Cuándo fue...?	*KWAHN-doh fway*
your last period	su última regla?	*soo OOL-tee-mah RAY-glah*
your last pap smear	su último Papanicolaou?	*soo OOL-tee-moh el pah-pah-nee-kohl-OW*
your last mammogram	su última mamograma?	*soo OOL-tee-mah mah-moh-GRAH-mah*
What do you use for birth control?	¿Qué tipo de anticonceptivo usa?	*kay TEE-poh day ahn-tee-cone-sape-TEE-boh OO-sah*
Have you had...?	¿Ha tenido...?	*ah tay-NEE-doh*
a sexually transmitted infection	alguna enfermedad de transmisión sexual?	*ahl-GOO-nah ain-fare-may-DAHD day trahns-mee-see-OWN sayk-soo-AHL*
an abnormal pap smear	un Papanicolaou anormal (malo)?	*oon pah-pah-nee-kohl-OW ah-nor-MAHL (MAH-loh)*
Is your period regular?	¿Es la regla normal cada mes?	*ase la RAY-glah nor-MAHL KAH-dah mace*
Is it light, medium, or heavy?	¿Es leve, normal, o abundante?	*ase LAY-bay, nor-MAHL, oh ah-boon-DAHN-tay*
Do you have cramps with your period?	¿Tiene cólicos o dolores menstruales con su regla?	*tee-AY-nay KOH-lee-kohs oh doh-LORE-ays mane-stroo-AH-lays cone soo RAY-glah*

Additional Words and Phrases:

OB/GYN – Pregnancy Questions

Have you ever been pregnant?	¿Alguna vez estuvo embarazada?	*ahl-GOO-nah base ay-STOO-boh ame-bah-rah-SAH-dah*
Are you pregnant now?	¿Está embarazada ahora?	*ay-STAH ame-bar-ah-SAH-dah ah-ORE-ah*
How many pregnancies have you had?	¿Cuántos embarazos ha tenido?	*KWAHN-tohs ame-bar-AH-sohs ah tay-NEE-doh*
Have you ever...?	¿Alguna vez...?	*ahl-GOO-nah base*
given birth...	dio a luz...	*dee-OH a loos*
naturally	por parto natural	*pore PAHR-toh nah-too-RAHL*
by Cesarean	por cesárea	*pore say-SAR-ee-ah*
had problems staying pregnant	tuvo problemas para quedar embarazada	*TOO-boh proh-BLAY-mahs PAH-rah kay-DAR ame-bar-ah-SAH-dah*
Have you had...?	¿Ha tenido...?	*ah tay-NEE-doh*
a miscarriage	un aborto espontáneo	*oon ah-BORE-toh ay-spone-TAH-nay-oh*
a stillborn	un niño que nació muerto	*oon NEE-nyoh kay nah-see-OH MWARE-toh*
an abortion	un aborto provocado	*oon ah-BORE-toh proh-boh-KAH-doh*
an ectopic (tubal) pregnancy	un embarazo ectópico (embarazo en la trompa)	*oon ame-bar-AH-soh ake-TOPE-ee-koh (ame-bar-AH-soh en la TROHM-pah)*
any operations	algunas operaciónes (cirugías)	*ahl-GOO-nahs oh-pare-ah-see-OWN-ays (see-roo-HEE-ahs)*

Additional Words and Phrases:

OB/GYN – Pregnancy Questions

When...?	¿Cuándo...?	*KWAHN-doh*
is your due date	será su fecha de parto	*sare-AH soo FAY-chah day PAR-toh*
was your first ultrasound	fue su primer ultrasonido?	*fway soo pree-MARE ool-trah-so-NEE-doh*

Have you...?	¿Ha..?	*ah*
had any problems with this pregnancy	tenido algún problema con éste embarazo	*tay-NEE-doh ahl-GOON proh-BLAY-mah cone AY-stay ame-bar-AH-soh*
had any bleeding	sangrado?	*sahn-GRAH-doh*
Was it pinkish or bright red?	¿Fue de color rosado o rojo?	*fway day koh-LORE roh-SAH-doh oh RO-hoh*

Do you have...?	¿Tiene..?	*tee-AY-nah*
pain	dolor	*doh-LORE*
preeclampsia symptoms	síntomas de preeclampsia	*SEEN-toh-mahs day pray-ay-KLAHMP-see-ah*
some pain or discomfort when you urinate	algún dolor o malestar cuando orina	*ahl-GOON doh-LORE oh mahl-ay-STAR KWAHN-doh oh-REE-nah*
vaginal bleeding	sangrado vaginal	*sahn-GRAH-doh bah-hee-NAHL*
contractions	dolores/contracciones	*doh-LORE-ays/cone-trahk-see-OWN-ays*

Additional Words and Phrases:

OB/GYN – Delivery

When did your contractions begin?	¿Cuándo comenzaron los dolores/las contracciones?	*KWAHN-doh koh-mane-SAR-own los doh-LORE-ays/las cone-trahk-see-OWN-ays*
How frequent are your contractions?	¿Con qué frecuencia son los dolores?	*cone kay fray-KWAY-see-ah sone los doh-LORE-ays*
What time did they become regular?	¿A qué hora empezaron a ser regulares (los dolores)?	*ah kay ORE-ah ame-pay-SAR-own ah sare ray-goo-LAR-ays (los doh-LORE-ays)*
How long do they last?	¿Cuánto le duran?	*KWAHN-toh lay DOO-rahn*
Did your membranes rupture?	¿Ha roto la bolsa de agua?	*ah ROH-toh la BOHL-sah day AH-gwah*
What time did it break?	¿A qué hora se rompió?	*ah kay ORE-ah say rohm-pee-OH*
Your cervix is not dilated.	Su cuello no está dilatado (abierto).	*soo KWAY-yoh no ay-STAH dee-lah-TAH-doh (ah-bee-AIR-toh).*
Your cervix is dilated to (3) centimeters.	Su cuello tiene (tres) centímetros de dilatación.	*soo KWAY-yoh tee-AY-nay (trace) sain-TEE-may-trohs day dee-lah-tah-see-OWN*
Push with your pains.	Empuje cuando sienta dolor.	*ame-POO-hay KWAHN-doh see-AIN-tah doh-LORE*
Don't push.	No empuje.	*no ame-POO-hay*
Breathe through your mouth.	Respire por la boca.	*ray-SPEER-ay pore la BOH-kah*
Congratulations! You have a baby girl (boy)!	¡Felicitaciones! ¡Es una niña (un niño)!	*fay-lee-see-tah-see-OWN-ay, ase OO-nah NEE-nyah (oon NEE-nyoh)*

Additional Words and Phrases:

Oncology

...cancer	cáncer (de...)	*KAHN-sare day*
breast	mama	*MAH-mah*
lung	pulmón	*pool-MOAN*
colon	colon	*KOH-lone*

leukemia	leucemia	*lay-oo-say-MEE-ah*
non-Hodgkin's lymphoma	linfoma no-Hodgkin	*leen-FOH-mah no-HOHG-keen*

We found...	Encontramos...	*ane-cone-TRAH-mohs*
an abnormality	una anormalidad	*OO-nah ah-nor-mahl-ee-DAHD*
a lump	un bulto	*oon BOOL-toh*
a lesion	una llaga	*OO-nah YAH-gah*
a spot	una mancha	*OO-nah MAHN-chah*
a bump	una protuberancia	*OO-nah proh-too-bare-AIN-see-ah*
a cyst	un quiste	*oon KEE-stay*
a tumor	un tumor	*oon too-MORE*

The cells are...	Las células son...	*las SALE-oo-lahs sown*
normal	normales	*nor-MAH-lays*
abnormal	anormales	*ah-nor-MAH-lays*
benign	benignas	*bay-NEEG-nahs*
malignant	malignas	*mahl-EEG-nahs*

The cells grow quickly.	Las células crecen rápidamente.	*las SALE-oo-lahs KRAY-sane RAH-pee-dah-MANE-tay*
The doctor needs a biopsy from your...	El médico necesita una biopsia de su...	*el MAY-dee-koh nay-say-SEE-tah OO-nah bee-OHP-see-ah day soo*

Additional Words and Phrases:

Optometry

astigmatism	astigmatismo	*ah-steeg-mah-TEES-moh*
blind	ciego/a	*see-AY-goh/ah*
cataracts	cataratas	*kah-tah-RAH-tahs*
color-blind	daltónico/a	*dahl-TOH-nee-koh/ah*
double vision	visión doble	*bee-see-OWN DOH-blay*
glaucoma	glaucoma	*glah-oo-KOH-mah*
You need...	Necesita...	*nay-say-SEE-tah*
a cataract operation	una operación de cataratas	*OO-nah oh-pare-ah-see-OWN day kah-tah-RAH-tahs*
a prescription	una prescripción	*OO-nah pray-skreep-see-OWN*
bifocals	bifocales	*bee-foh-KAHL-ays*
contact lenses	lentes de contacto	*LANE-tays day cone-TAHK-toh*
eye drops	gotas para los ojos	*GOH-tahs PAH-rah los OH-hohs*
glasses	lentes	*LANE-tays*
laser surgery	cirugía con láser	*see-roo-HEE-ah cone LAH-sare*
new frames	armazones nuevos	*ar-mah-SOHN-ays NWAY-bohs*
reading glasses	lentes para leer	*LANE-tayes PAH-rah lay-AIR*
Cover your eye.	Tape el ojo.	*TAH-pay el OH-hoh*
Look here.	Mire aquí.	*MEER-ay ah-KEY*
Look up and down.	Mire hacia arriba y abajo.	*MEER-ay AH-see-ah ah-REE-bah ee ah-BAH-hoh*
Read this.	Lea esto.	*LAY-ah AY-stoh*
Don't blink.	No parpadee.	*no par-pah-DAY-ay*
Is it...?	¿Está...?	*ay-STAH*
better	mejor	*may-HORE*
clear	claro	*KLAR-oh*
blurry	borroso	*bore-OH-soh*
worse	peor	*pay-ORE*

Additional Words and Phrases:

Physical and Occupational Therapy

Do you use equipment to help you walk?	¿Usa aparatos para caminar?	OO-sah ah-par-AH-tohs PAH-rah kah-mee-NAR
walker	el andador	el ahn-dah-DOOR
rolling walker	el andador con ruedas	el anh-dah-DOOR cone roo-AY-dahs
cane	el bastón	el bah-STOHN
splint	la tablilla	la tah-BLEE-yah
crutches	las muletas	las moo-LAY-tahs
wheelchair	la silla de ruedas	la SEE-yah day roo-AY-dahs

What is your...?	¿Cuál es...?	KWAHL es
severity of injury	la severidad de la lesión	la say-bare-ee-DAHD day la lay-see-OWN
time since injury	el tiempo desde la lesión	el tee-AIM-poh DAYS-day la lay-see-OWN
level of injury	el nivel de la lesión	el nee-BALE day la lay-see-OWN
level of fitness	el nivel de la condición física	el nee-BALE day la cone-dee-see-OWN FEE-see-kah
level of sensation	el nivel de la sensibilidad	el nee-BALE day la sane-see-bee-lee-DAHD
level of pain	el nivel del dolor	el nee-BALE del doh-LORE

Additional Words and Phrases:

Physical and Occupational Therapy

Can he/she/you ...?	¿Puede...?	PWAY-day
bathe	bañarse	bah-NYAR-say
cook	cocinar	koh-see-NAR
do household chores	hacer quehaceres domésticos	ah-SARE kay-ah-SARE-ays
drive	conducir / manejar	cone-doo-SEER / mah-nay-HAR
eat	comer	koh-MARE
get dressed	vestirse	bay-STEER-say
get ready	arreglarse	ah-ray-GLAR-say
go shopping	ir de compras	eer day KOHM-prahs
go up stairs	subir escaleras	soo-BEER ay-skah-LARE-ahs
manage his/her/your...	manejar su...	mah-nay-HAR soo
... oral hygiene	...higiene bucal	ee-hee-ANE-ay boo-KAHL
...medication	...medicamentos	may-dee-kah-MAIN-tohs
...finances	...finanzas	fee-NAHN-sahs
use the bathroom	usar el baño	oo-SAR el BAH-nyoh
use the telephone	usar el teléfono	oo-SAR el tay-LAY-foh-noh
walk	caminar	kah-mee-NAR
wash the clothes	lavar la ropa	la-BAR la ROH-poh
Are there stairs in your house or apartment?	¿Hay escaleras en su casa o apartamento?	eye ay-skah-LARE-ahs en soo KAH-sah oh ah-par-tah-MANE-toh
I would like to test your strength.	Me gustaría examinar su fuerza.	may goo-star-EE-ah ayk-sah-may-NAR soo FWARE-sah

Additional Words and Phrases:

Pharmacy Instructions

You need...	Necesita...	*nay-say-SEE-tah*
an antibiotic	un antibiótico	*oon ahn-tee-bee-OO-tee-koh*
medicine	medicina	*may-dee-SEE-nah*
vitamins	vitaminas	*bee-tah-MEE-nahs*
Take the medicine...	Tome la medicina...	*TOH-may la may-dee-SEE-nah*
when you wake up	al levantarse	*ahl lay-bahn-TAR-say*
after meals	despúes de las comidas	*day-SPWAYS day las koh-MEE-dahs*
before meals	antes de las comidas	*AHN-tays day las koh-MEE-dahs*
between meals	entre las comidas	*AIN-tray las koh-MEE-dahs*
at bedtime	al acostarse	*ahl ah-koh-STAR-say*
for (10) days	por (10) días	*pore (dee-AYS) DEE-ahs*
when you have pain	cuando tenga dolor	*KWAHN-doh TANE-gah doh-LORE*
with water ___	con agua ___	*cone AH-gwah __ BAY-says*
times every ___	veces cada ___	*KAH-dah __*
Take...	Tome...	*TOH-may*
a cup	una copa	*OO-nah KOH-pah*
a glass	un vaso	*oon BAH-soh*
half	la mitad	*la mee-TAHD*
one tablespoon	una cucharada	*OO-nah koo-char-AH-dah*
one teaspoon	una cucharadita	*OO-nah koo-char-ah-DEE-tah*
You have to...	Tiene que...	*tee-AY-nay kay*
measure carefully	medir con cuidado	*may-DEER cone KWEE-dah-doh*
read the label	leer la etiqueta	*lay-AIR la ay-tee-KAY-tah*
refrigerate it	refrigerarlo	*ray-free-hair-AR-low*

Additional Words and Phrases:

Pharmacy – Kinds of Medicine

Take...	Tome...	TOH-may
half of...	la mitad de...	*la mee-TAHD day*
one tablespoon	una cucharada	*OO-nah koo-char-AH-dah*
one teaspoon	una cucharadita	*OO-nah koo-char-ah-DEE-tah*
½ teaspoon	media cucharadita	*MAY-dee-ah koo-char-ah-DEE-tah*
milligrams (mg)	miligramos	*mee-lee-GRAH-mohs*
milliliters (ml)	mililitros	*mee-lee-LEE-trohs*
a glass	un vaso	*oon BAH-soh*
capsule	la cápsula	*la KAHP-soo-lah*
cream	la crema	*la KRAY-mah*
dropper	el gotero	*el goh-TARE-oh*
drops	las gotas	*las GOH-tahs*
gel	el gel	*el hale*
intravenous (IV)	intravenoso	*een-trah-bay-NOH-soh*
liquid	el líquido	*el LEE-kee-doh*
lotion	la loción	*la loh-see-OWN*
ointment	la pomad/el ungüento	*la poh-MAH-dah/el oon-GWAIN-toh*
pill	la pastilla	*la pah-STEE-yah*
powder	el polvo	*el POHL-boh*
suppository	el supositorio	*el soo-poh-see-TORE-ee-oh*
syringe	la jeringa	*la hare-EEN-gah*
syrup	el jarabe	*el har-AH-bay*
tablet	la tableta	*la tah-BLAY-tah*

Additional Words and Phrases:

Pulmonology - Vocabulary

trachea	la tráquea	*la TRAH-kay-ah*
lungs	los pulmones	*los pool-MOH-nays*
sinuses	los senos	*los SAY-nohs*
larynx	la laringe	*la lah-REEN-hay*
mouth	la boca	*la BOH-kah*
epiglottis	la epiglotis	*la ay-pee-GLOH-tees*
esophagus	el esófago	*el ay-SOH-fah-goh*
bronchi	los bronquios	*los BROHN-kee-ohs*
alveoli	los alvéolos pulmonares	*los ahl-BAY-oh-lohs pool-moh-NAR-ays*
pleura	la pleura	*la play-OO-rah*
nostril	la fosa nasal	*la FOH-sah nah-SAHL*
diaphragm	el diafragma	*el dee-ah-FRAHG-mah*

Additional Words and Phrases:

Pulmonology - Questions

Have you had…?	¿Ha tenido…?	*ah tay-NEE-doh*
an asthma attack	un ataque de asma	*oon ah-TAH-kay day AH-smah*
emphysema	enfisema	*ane-fee-SAY-mah*
bronchitis	bronquitis	*brohn-KEE-tees*
pneumonia	pulmonía / neumonía	*pool-moh-NEE-ah / nay-oo-moh-NEE-ah*
Do you have…	¿Tiene…?	*tee-AY-nay*
allergies	alergias	*ah-LARE-hee-ahs*
asthma	asma	*AH-smah*
difficulty breathing	dificultad al respirar	*dee-fee-kool-TAHD ahl ray-speer-AR*
difficulty sleeping	dificultad para dormir	*dee-fee-kool-TAHD PAH-rah doh-MEER*
chills	escalofríos	*ay-skah-loh-FREE-ohs*
sputum	esputo	*ay-SPOO-toh*
shortness of breath	falta de aire	*FAHL-tah day EYE-ray*
exhaustion	fatiga	*fah-TEE-gah*
phlegm	flema	*FLAY-mah*
hiccups	hipo	*EE-poh*
frequent colds	resfriados frecuentes	*ray-sfree-AH-dohs fray-KWAIN-tays*
secretion	secreción	*say-kray-see-OWN*
wheezing	silbido al respirar	*seel-BAH-doh ahl ray-speer-AR*
cough	tos	*tohs*
Do you smoke?	¿Fuma?	*FOO-mah*
How many packs a day?	¿Cuántas cajetillas al día?	*KWAHN-tahs kah-hay-TEE-yahs ahl DEE-ah*
For how long?	¿Por cuánto tiempo?	*pore KWAHN-toh tee-AIM-poh*

Additional Words and Phrases:

Radiology

CT scan	el tomógrafo	*el toh-MOH-grah-foh*
machine	la máquina	*la MAH-kee-nah*
mammography	mamografía	*mah-moh-grah-FEE-ah*
MRI scan	Imágenes por Resonancia Magnética (IRM)	*ee-MAH-hay-nays pore ray-soh-NAHN-see-ah mahg-NAY-tee-kah*
NM scan	examen de medicina nuclear	*ayk-SAH-mane day may-dee-SEE-ah noo-klay-AR*
PET scan	tomografía por emisión de positrones (TEP)	*toh-moh-grah-FEE-ah pore ay-mee-see-OWN day poh-see-TRONE-ays*
screen	la pantalla	*la pahn-TIE-yah*
ultrasound	ultrasonido	*ool-trah-so-NEE-doh*
X-ray	radiografía, rayos x (equis), placa	*rah-dee-oh-grah-FEE-ah, RAH-yohs AY-keys, PLAH-kah*
Put this gown on, with the opening toward the front.	Póngase esta bata, con la abertura hacia adelante.	*PONE-gah-say AY-stah BAH-tah, cone la ah-bare-TOO-rah AH-see-ah ah-day-LAHN-tay*
Let me know when you are ready.	Avíseme cuando esté listo/a.	*ah-BEE-say-may KWAHN-doh ay-STAY LEE-stoh/ah*
Undress (only the area of your chest).	Desvístase (sólo la parte del pecho).	*days-BEE-stah-say (soh-loh la PAR-tay del PAY-choh)*
Hold the position.	Mantenga la posición.	*mahn-TANE-gah la poh-see-see-OWN*
Don't move.	No se mueva.	*no say MWAY-bah*
Very good. You are in position.	Muy bien. Está en posición.	*MWEE bee-ANE ay-STAH ane po-see-see-OWN*

Additional Words and Phrases:

Online Courses

Do you want to hear how these words are pronounced?
Would you like more individual practice?

Individuals or groups may also want to supplement this guide with one of our self-paced online courses. The online courses, *Pronto Spanish Fundamentals* or *Pronto Spanish for Medical Professionals* at www.OpenSesame.com, covers very similar vocabulary, yet gives students additional practice with games, pictures, readings, native-speaker pronunciations, cultural tidbits, quick grammar tips, and quizzes.

For a larger online learning community with a Discussion Area and access to an instructor to ask all of your questions, visit www.ed2go.com and search for *Spanish for Medical Professionals* and *Spanish for Medical Professionals II*.

About the Author

Tara Bradley Williams, co-founder of Pronto Spanish, is the author and instructional designer for all Pronto Spanish books, online courses, and materials. Tara has over 20 years of Spanish and ELL (English Language Learner) teaching experience in K-12 public schools, community college, and corporate training levels and has studied, lived, and traveled extensively in Spain and Latin America. She currently lives and works in Wisconsin with her husband and three children.

Pronto Spanish® has been delivering high quality Spanish courses, curriculum, and online courses since 2002. The goal of Pronto Spanish is to help adult students learn the Spanish basics and job-specific Spanish vocabulary to help them better communicate in the workplace.

www.ProntoSpanish.com
Twitter: @ProntoSpanish
Facebook: www.facebook.com/ProntoSpanishServices